THE LITTLE BOOK OF

RESTORATIVE JUSTICE IN EDUCATION

Published titles include:

The Little Book of Restorative Justice: Revised & Updated,
by Howard Zehr

The Little Book of Conflict Transformation,
by John Paul Lederach

The Little Book of Family Group Conferences,
New-Zealand Style, by Allan MacRae and Howard Zehr

The Little Book of Strategic Peacebuilding, by Lisa Schirch

The Little Book of Strategic Negotiation,
by Jayne Seminare Docherty

The Little Book of Circle Processes, by Kay Pranis

The Little Book of Contemplative Photography, by Howard Zehr

The Little Book of Restorative Discipline for Schools,
by Lorraine Stutzman Amstutz and Judy H. Mullet

The Little Book of Trauma Healing, by Carolyn Yoder

The Little Book of Biblical Justice, by Chris Marshall

The Little Book of Restorative Justice for People in Prison,
by Barb Toews

The Little Book of Cool Tools for Hot Topics,
by Ron Kraybill and Evelyn Wright

El Pequeño Libro De Justicia Restaurativa, by Howard Zehr

The Little Book of Dialogue, by Lisa Schirch and David Campt

The Little Book of Victim Offender Conferencing,
by Lorraine Stutzman Amstutz

The Little Book of Restorative Justice for Sexual Abuse, by Judah
Oudshoorn with Michelle Jackett and Lorraine Stutzman Amstutz

The Big Book of Restorative Justice: Three Classic Justice &
Peacebuilding Books in One Volume, by Howard Zehr, Lorraine S.
Amstutz, Allan Macrae, and Kay Pranis

The Little Book of Transformative Community Conferencing, by
David Anderson Hooker

The Little Books of Justice & Peacebuilding present,
in highly accessible form, key concepts and practices from
the fields of restorative justice, conflict transformation, and
peacebuilding. Written by leaders in these fields, they are
designed for practitioners, students, and anyone interested in
justice, peace, and conflict resolution.

The Little Books of Justice & Peacebuilding series is
a cooperative effort between the Center for Justice and
Peacebuilding of Eastern Mennonite University and publisher
Good Books.

THE LITTLE BOOK OF
RESTORATIVE JUSTICE IN EDUCATION

Fostering Responsibility, Healing, and Hope in Schools

KATHERINE EVANS AND
DOROTHY VAANDERING

Good Books
NEW YORK, NEW YORK

Good Books books may be purchased in bulk at special discounts for sales promotion, corporate gifts, fund-raising, or educational purposes. Special editions can also be created to specifications. For details, contact the Special Sales Department, Good Books, 207 West 36th Street, 11th Floor, New York, NY 10018 or info@skyhorsepublishing.com.

Good Books is an imprint of Skyhorse Publishing, Inc.®, a Delaware corporation.

Visit our website at www.goodbooks.com

10 9 8 7 6 5 4 3 2 1

Library of Congress Cataloging-in-Publication Data is available on file.

ISBN: 978-1-68099-172-7
e-ISBN: 978-1-68099-173-4

Printed in the United States of America

Acknowledgments

The content of this book is not our own. There are many who have informed our understanding and practice of restorative justice in education and brought us to this point of authoring this book.

In particular, we are indebted to the humility and grace offered by indigenous peoples across North America who have kept the wonder of circle dialogue alive through generations while threatened with genocide.

We trust that this Little Book honors indigenous teachers and traditions and further opens our hearts—settler-Canadians and settler-Americans—to be still and learn more fully from their wisdom so generously offered.

Table of Contents

Preface

Restorative justice (RJ), as articulated in Western contexts, has been gaining traction in multiple arenas. For example, communities are using the principles of RJ to build healthy interactions among neighbors. Juvenile and adult legal systems have incorporated RJ into diversion programs and reparation options. Prisons have initiated reentry programs based on RJ principles to support people post-incarceration.

Restorative justice is also making inroads in education. Educators, since the late 1990s, have been conducting circle processes to nurture classrooms and school communities, initiating reentry programs for students suspended or expelled, and using RJ principles and practices for responding to challenging behaviors and harms. The growth in the field of RJ as applied to educational settings is a result of many educators working diligently to implement its principles and practices into the daily life of a school. Various publications have supported and encouraged growth in the field, including two Little Books—*The Little Book of Circle Processes* by Kay Pranis (2005) and *The Little Book of Restorative Discipline for Schools* by Lorraine Stutzman Amstutz and Judy Mullet (2005). Since those publications, experience, reflection, and research have affirmed much of their content. New insights have also emerged.

Perhaps the greatest insight gained over the years is that restorative justice implemented in educational environments is primarily about nurturing relational, interconnected school cultures. While some early engagement with RJ may have acknowledged the broader health of the school environment, the predominant focus was on individual discipline and behavior. It is now evident that addressing discipline and harmful behavior apart from the context of community interconnectedness, while maintaining a hierarchical power structure often found in schools, will be ineffective.

To deepen our understanding of the nature of restorative justice in education (RJE), a stronger theoretical framework is developing. To date, restorative justice has primarily been a grassroots movement with practice, rather than theory, driving its growth. This has allowed for the development of intricate practice, but as RJE matures, clearly articulated theory becomes necessary for RJ practices to be effective and sustainable. For example, without a well-articulated theory, it is difficult to address concerns such as why some schools have been able to develop and sustain their practice while others have not. A consistent theoretical foundation for RJE is necessary as educators continue to search for approaches to building healthy communities in light of the following trends:

(a) The growing rejection of exclusionary discipline and zero-tolerance policies that are seen to perpetuate student apathy, disproportionality,[1] and the school-to-prison pipeline.

(b) Recent research studies that are identifying restorative justice in education as having significant potential for schools.[2]

Finally, a strong theoretical framework will help to prevent restorative justice practices from being misunderstood, diluted, or misused in ways that could actually create further harm.

In summary, RJE as presented in this Little Book explores the phrase *restorative justice in education* and then expands to identify three major interconnected and equally important concepts:

- *Creating just and equitable learning environments.*
- *Nurturing healthy relationships.*
- *Repairing harm and transforming conflict.*

Stories, examples, and brief exercises will be used throughout this book to demonstrate how these concepts can be practiced.

Like a compass whose needle points us toward our destination, theory guides our practice.[3] A reference point that practitioners can return to when the daily challenges of school arise is necessary to ensure clarity and consistency. Without it, there is a strong temptation to revert back to the punitive, rewards-based approaches that school systems have unsuccessfully relied on.

The Little Book of Restorative Justice in Education serves as this compass needle. Relying on the wisdom of early proponents of restorative justice, the daily experiences of educators, and our own extensive experience as classroom teachers and researchers, we have created a guide that we hope will point toward and support the growth of RJE into the future.

SECTION 1
Preparing for
Sustainable Growth

R estorative justice in education (RJE) has had a relatively short history through which various principles and practices have emerged. In Section 1, we carefully outline an overview of RJE (Chapter 1), its growth over time (Chapter 2), and the beliefs and values that support sustainable implementation in educational settings (Chapter 3). We liken the growth of RJE to that of a plant. This analogy is introduced as a way to illustrate the intricate (and beautiful!) process of organic growth. We trust the comparison will help explain concepts that are often overlooked—much like an established, growing root system that lies below the surface, allowing us to enjoy the beauty of a plant or tree.

Chapter 1:
The Way We Do Things

Restorative justice in education (RJE) is alive in story.

1. The stuffed bear is passed around a circle of
   twenty-one fourth-grade students. It comes to
   Joey, a student with communication challenges,
   who holds it in silence. After several moments, a
   few peers encourage him to speak or pass it on.
   The teacher stops them and reminds the group
   that holding the talking piece in silence is a way
   of communicating. Joey smiles appreciatively and
   then passes the bear. In the next round, two of
   the other students hold the bear in silence. Joey
   relaxes his tensed shoulders.
2. The group of students approaches Ms. Gonzales,
   confused about the final assignment. They have
   worked hard yet made little progress. She is
   tempted to explain for the fourth time what
   is expected. She stops instead to listen as they
   respond to her questions: What is happening?
   What are you thinking/feeling about the work?
   What is the hardest thing for each of you? What

impact is this having on you? What do you need from me to move forward?

3. The two ninth-grade girls, once friends, have been quarreling for days. Today, the guidance counselor takes them aside and creates a safe space for them to talk. Responding to guiding questions, the girls explain their experience, their thoughts and feelings, and the impact their situation is causing. They then thoughtfully identify what they need, and what they can offer, to move forward.

The outcome of each of these stories is like a flowering plant. Looking closely at flowers, we see beauty and complexity, a completeness that makes us wonder at their intricacy. In awe of the blooms, we rarely consider the seed that started off in darkness, or the roots under the soil supporting and feeding the plant. When we cut off the flower and put it in water, we know we can enjoy it for a few days; however, without the roots, it cannot complete its bloom and set seed for another flower.

The Purpose of This Book

The purpose of this Little Book is to direct attention to the seed, the root structure, and the supporting branches holding up the positive experiences arising from the implementation of RJE. With a strong understanding of its theory and philosophy, the practice of RJE can be further nurtured and strengthened. Also, when at times it fails to thrive, we may be able to identify the reason this failure happened.

The three opening stories reflect three interconnected components of RJE that have grown up over years of practice in schools:

- *Creating just and equitable learning environments*
- *Nurturing healthy relationships*
- *Repairing harm and transforming conflict*

These components have grown from core beliefs (seeds) that *people are worthy and relational,* and are rooted in values of *respect, dignity,* and *mutual concern.*

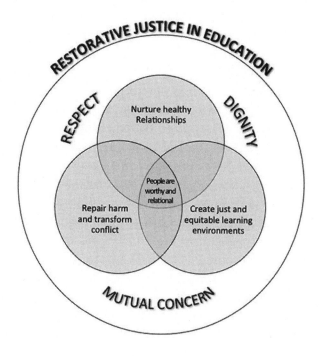

Figure 1.1

As educators have engaged with RJE in their various contexts, the hope they experience from it is often intertwined with questions, concerns, and misunderstandings. In this book we endeavor to build on the early, current, and growing literature available for educators to nurture the ever-expanding potential of RJE. As teacher educators, we offer our insights from extensive classroom and research experience, as well as personal commitment to the essence of restorative justice (RJ) that has grown over the years. We see great benefit in connecting RJE to teaching and learning theory, as well as to school climate and culture. When placed carefully and purposefully in these educational contexts, the roots of restorative justice grow deeper and stronger.

What Is RJE?

Early forms of restorative justice in education borrowed from judicial settings. As a result, schools often adopted restorative justice similarly as a strategy to address behavioral issues, resolve conflict, and address harm. However, when restorative justice circle conferencing was employed in schools and facilitated with care and consistency, the significance of interconnected relationships became evident. Repairing harms required more than involving those directly affected by an incident. RJ became a shared responsibility, a commitment to creating just and equitable learning environments. In these holistic responses, RJE advocates were challenged first to rethink their assumptions about *justice, restorative,* and *education,* and then to consider how RJ was being implemented in the institutional structure of a school. (See Chapter 2 for details regarding the history of RJE.)

Definitions

Restorative justice in education encompasses a variety of terms and approaches. Some of the most common include restorative practices, restorative discipline, restorative approaches, restorative measures, and restorative justice practices. Alongside these, forms of peer mediation, social-emotional learning (SEL), peacebuilding, and antibullying programs also share some goals of RJE for improving school climate, safety, and learning. How do we understand these overlapping approaches, and how might RJE bring together the strongest elements of each?

The phrase *restorative justice in education* synthesizes and amplifies what is shared among the perspectives, pointing us in a clearer direction. In this book, the terms *justice, restorative,* and *education* are defined as follows:

Justice honors the inherent worth of all. It is enacted through relationships. Primary justice, sometimes called social justice, is the condition of respect, dignity, and the protection of rights and opportunities for all, existing in relationships where no one is wronged. Secondary justice, or judicial justice, is understood mainly as a response to harm or crime.[1]

Restorative, as an adjective for both primary and secondary justice, describes how an individual's or group's dignity, worth, and interconnectedness will be nurtured, protected, or reestablished in ways that will allow people to be fully contributing members of their communities.

Education comes from the Latin word *educare,* meaning "to lead out, to draw out." Therefore, it includes learning in all contexts, formal and informal, and seeks to empower learners of all ages to live out their capacity for being human and relational.

Each of these words on its own presumes and reflects a view of human beings as unique and full of potential. When combined, the term *restorative justice in education* can be defined as

facilitating learning communities that nurture the capacity of people to engage with one another and their environment in a manner that supports and respects the inherent dignity and worth of all.

Ultimately RJE is a vision of education that acknowledges that our individual and collective well-being is enhanced less through personal striving than through collective engagement and support.

RJE: The Way We Do Things Around Here

When restorative justice is understood holistically, it intersects with educational institutions from preschool to university in ways that stimulate cultural norms—"the way we do things around here." It is important to recognize that the *culture* of a school grows out of people's beliefs and values. In the busyness of life and learning, these are often assumed, rarely discussed, and regularly misunderstood. Implementing RJE is most successful when time is taken to identify and commit to certain core beliefs and values. What are these core beliefs and values?

Returning to the diagram (Figure 1.1), we can see these more clearly.

The *core beliefs* of RJE are that all human beings are worthy and interconnected. RJE recognizes people's need to belong or the "universal human wish to be connected to others in a good way."[2] These beliefs are supported by three key *values*: respect, dignity, and mutual concern. Within these values, a variety of others can also be identified based on the differing needs of people. For example, suppose that to be at your best when you are with others, *trust, honesty,* and *encouragement* are three things you value. However, a peer may identify that *responsibility, promptness,* and *humor* are key values required for the peer to feel worthy and interconnected. What is important for our discussion of RJE is that

- beliefs and values nurture the well-being of self and others, and
- well-being involves the whole of the educational experience.

Chapter 3 discusses the underlying beliefs and core values of RJE in more detail. Chapters 4–6 discuss the following three necessary components of restorative school cultures.

Creating just and equitable learning environments means that all students and staff will be acknowledged and accepted for who they are, including their race, gender, sexuality, socioeconomic status, religion, language, etc. Everyone should have the opportunity to participate in providing and receiving resources and support for their own and others' learning experiences so that they can each experience life to its fullest extent. Ultimately, the purpose of RJE is to create spaces of belonging that embrace everyone in the ways they require. This involves the use of culturally responsive pedagogy and curriculum, diverse instructional approaches, social-emotional learning, explicit ongoing engagement with human rights concepts in all curriculum, and social interaction that embodies justice and equity *not* as equal distribution of resources but as the respectful meeting of needs.

Nurturing healthy relationships acknowledges that social and emotional health is critical for learning and living. Students and educators alike thrive when they feel accepted and respected by those nearby. Thus respect, inclusion, conflict resolution, reciprocal learning and teaching, decision making, etc., are integrated within all aspects of education—i.e., curriculum, pedagogy, hallway interactions, lunchroom and bus environments, administrative and policy protocol, staff meetings, and family-school engagement.

Repairing harm and transforming conflict acknowledges that conflict and harm are a normal part of life and often provide opportunities for learning and transformation. Together, all involved in the community learn to communicate clearly in order to identify harms, to encourage accountability for those who have caused harm, and to accept and address the needs of those harmed and those causing harm.

To be sustainable, RJE must be understood holistically. Without explicit engagement with core beliefs and values, there will be no reference point to return to when the way becomes unclear or confused. If a school chooses to focus only on restorative justice as a practice to address incidents of harm while ignoring the learning environment and nurturing healthy relationships, it is possible that agreements reached for addressing harm (usually an outcome of RJ practices) will not be sustainable and may actually cause further harm. If the focus is on nurturing and maintaining healthy relationships and encouraging interconnected classrooms and school communities, but responses to inappropriate behavior are primarily punitive and rewards-driven, students will experience a double standard that undermines their sense of worth and well-being. In the same way, if emphasis is given to creating just and equitable learning environments, but the curriculum ignores the race or religion of some students while privileging others, trust—an essential element of just relationships—will be undermined. Ultimately, a commitment to honoring the worth and interconnectedness of human beings must be evident in all areas of education.

How Is RJE Different from Traditional Education?

For decades, many educational philosophers and theorists have encouraged relational engagement (e.g., Dewey, Vygotsky, Freire, Noddings, Kohn). In that regard, RJE is not new. RJE is an expression of the communities of care and respect that theorists and philosophers have historically encouraged in schools. However, new perspectives take time to take root in culture. Though education provides significant hope, it also serves as a means for social control, where students are taught to comply and to take up their place in an economy-driven world. In spite of significant effort over time to change this, policies and practices that continue to be most popular are those that industrialize schooling and undermine the well-being of individuals and their communities (e.g., zero tolerance; economic defunding of public education and inequitable distribution of resources; standardized grade levels, curriculum, and testing; and rewards-based learning).[3]

RJE is an invitation to create educational cultures that emphasize social engagement rather than social control.[4] The starting point in "how we are when we are together" is relationships rather than rules, people rather than policies, honoring capacity rather than evaluating ability, creating meaning rather than imposing knowledge, asking rather than telling, and well-being rather than merit-based success. This does not imply that rules, policies, evaluation, telling, and success are irrelevant; it simply means that these serve the needs of people living within community, not the other way around. RJE holds the possibility for changing learning factories into gardens where seeds are planted and growth is nurtured.

Summary

At its heart, RJE invites educators to *engage with* students, students' parents/caregivers, colleagues, curriculum, and educational institutions in a way that *honors* individuals in the context of their communities. In this way, as individuals and communities, everyone can thrive and grow to their full potential. As with any living entity, engagement requires shared caregiving and empowerment that *nurtures, feeds, guides,* and *supports.* It challenges traditional hierarchical power dynamics that expect educators to *manage, control, shape,* or *mold* students, as if they were inanimate objects. RJE creates spaces of shared learning and teaching.

Chapter 2:
A Brief History of Restorative Justice in Education

The task of writing a history of restorative justice in education (RJE) seems daunting. On one hand, the field is very young. On the other hand, its history is embedded within the field of restorative justice (RJ), which has a long history. RJE's history, while short, is also complex, emerging from grassroots work all over the globe. Complicating RJE's history is the concurrent rise of a whole host of programs, processes, and fields that also seek to provide more holistic ways of doing education. While some of these might not use the language of RJ, they align with the principles of RJE and many have since morphed into RJE projects.

Despite the difficulty of the task, we believe that understanding the historical roots of RJE will enable the field to move forward in more constructive ways. We acknowledge that our telling is an incomplete history, bound by our own perspectives and experiences. It simply provides a starting point. Thus, in this chapter, we will attempt to outline a history of RJE while acknowledging that (1) there is much localized work that has been unwritten, and (2) in our selection of what to include in this chapter, we are presenting only one possible historical narrative.

The Restorative Justice Foundations of RJE

Restorative justice, as a field, began in the criminal justice system. However, the principles of RJ predate Western society. For example, peacemaking circles within non-Western communities have long served as spaces for solving the problems of the community *within the community.* Indigenous communities such as the Navajo people have historically viewed harm and conflict as a symptom of disconnection and have viewed justice through a lens of healing and reconnection— a restoration of relationships. Likewise, Maori tribes in New Zealand have incorporated community-based sentencing and family group conferencing into their community practices for generations. These traditional approaches to peacebuilding and conflict resolution have been documented in other sources, and we rely on those authors for the early history of restorative justice.[1]

The Elmira Case of 1974 is generally considered the first Western application of restorative justice principles. Sometimes called the Kitchener Experiment, due to its roots in Kitchener, Ontario, Canada, this case began what became known as victim-offender reconciliation programs (VORP), which sought to find alternatives for addressing harm and responding to crime in ways that focused on relationships and healing rather than simply laws and punishment.

In the Elmira case, a Canadian probation officer and a volunteer with the Mennonite Central Committee tried a more community-focused approach to a case involving two young men charged with vandalism. The two men were given the opportunity to meet with their victims and provide restitution. The outcome was a success. Modeled after the Elmira case, other victim-offender reconciliation programs were developed, initially within the criminal justice system and then within the juvenile justice system. VORP was introduced in the United States in Elkhart, Indiana, in the mid-1970s under the leadership of Howard Zehr, who has been a leader in the field of restorative justice for more than forty years. In 1990, Zehr authored *Changing Lenses: A New Focus for Crime and Justice,* now considered a seminal text of restorative justice, in which he provided a theoretical grounding for the growing work. Restorative justice continued to gain traction, becoming officially recognized by the American Bar Association in 1994 and by the United Nations in 1999.[2]

Expanding to the Educational Arena

The application of restorative justice principles and practices in schools is relatively new, with its early recorded work primarily in Australia, New Zealand, Canada, the United States, and the United Kingdom. While RJ was growing in the criminal justice arena, teachers, principals, and counselors began applying practices that had been found effective in the judicial system and adapting them to fit more closely with school contexts. For example, in 2000, a restorative justice partnership in British Columbia, Canada, emerged between the Community Justice Initiatives Association and the Langley School District, bringing the practices of RJ into schools. Similar community-school partnerships emerged across the globe, including in Pennsylvania and Colorado (USA), Queensland (Australia), Oxfordshire (England), and Wellington (New Zealand).

During this period of growth, Wendy Drewery (New Zealand) and Marg Thorsborne (Australia), as well as many others, built on indigenous (Maori) practices and led the way in implementing family group conferences in school settings. Singapore and other parts of Asia also initiated peer mediation programs to address conflict and bullying, and the Safer School Partnerships arose in the United Kingdom, building on the restorative initiatives already being developed in schools by Belinda Hopkins and others since the mid-1990s.

The state of Minnesota (USA), under the leadership of Nancy Riestenberg, was a front-runner of restorative justice in school settings. Between 1998 and 2001, the Minnesota Department of Children, Families, and Learning began to work with schools to reduce suspensions and expulsions through the implementation of what were called restorative measures. Spurred on by the successes the schools were experiencing, the restorative justice work in Minnesota continued to grow into a statewide effort under the auspices of the Minnesota Department of Education (MN DoE). Riestenberg was hired by the MN DoE as a school climate specialist, responsible for supporting the implementation of restorative justice in Minnesota schools. Minnesota continues to embed restorative justice into school policies and practices and has provided a model for other schools, districts, and states seeking to implement RJE. During the mid-2000s, several districts in Ontario, Canada (e.g., Waterloo, York), began hiring people to oversee the implementation of restorative justice practices in schools. Lynn Zammit, Angie Dornai, Brenda Morrison, and Jennifer Llewellyn were some of the early leaders in the RJE movement in Canada.

In addition, a local Pennsylvania nonprofit, applying restorative justice principles in its work with students who had been expelled from school, established SaferSanerSchools in 1999. Out of that work, the International Institute for Restorative Practices (IIRP) emerged. The IIRP developed the first graduate-level program, accredited in 2007, that exclusively focused on teaching restorative practices. Besides developing its graduate school, the IIRP has established branches in Australia, Canada, Europe, and South America.

One of the things that complicates any attempt to devise a history of RJE is the number of other programs, such as peace education, conflict resolution education, peer mediation, and restitution, that were also being developed to resolve school-based conflicts, to address the relational and learning needs of students, and to promote peacebuilding in schools. Throughout the 1980s and 1990s, before the term *restorative justice* had found its way into schools, these programs had been functioning effectively. As the language of restorative justice trickled into schools, the mingling of restorative justice with already existing programs was inevitable and, in many contexts, paved the way for restorative justice to grow.

Columbine, Taber, and the Era of Zero Tolerance

Even as restorative justice was finding its way into schools, so were zero-tolerance policies. In 1994, the Gun-Free Schools Act (GFSA) was passed in the US, and the Safe Schools Act (SSA) was passed in Canada in 2000. The concept of zero tolerance had been connected to the criminal justice system for years, representing a "get tough on crime" mentality. With the GFSA and the SSA, the language of zero tolerance found its way into schools, creating more draconian approaches to school discipline. Initially, policies in both countries called for mandatory suspensions for any weapons possession on school campuses; eventually it was expanded to include drug possessions and a host of other offenses.

In 1999, two events led to a full-scale ramping up of those draconian measures: On April 20, in Columbine, Colorado, USA, two students opened fire at Columbine High School, killing thirteen and injuring twenty-one others. Eight days later, a fourteen-year-old student walked into a high school in Taber, Alberta, Canada, and shot another youth in what appeared to be an attempt to replicate the Columbine attack. In the years following those two school shootings, the application of zero-tolerance policies escalated to include a host of school behaviors, increasing the use of suspensions and expulsions and laying the foundation for what has often been called the school-to-prison pipeline.[3] In fact, the "zero-tolerance frenzy"[4] seemed to have backfired to some extent; after a few years, the general population began to seriously question the effectiveness of zero-tolerance policies, and many schools began to back off of some of the more extreme applications.

From Zero Tolerance to Restorative Justice

The mid-2000s saw an increase in the criticism of zero-tolerance policies. Critiques made way for new restorative justice initiatives. For example, in 2007, the Minister of Education for Ontario in Canada announced that zero tolerance had been a failure and initiated legislation that would replace zero-tolerance policies with student supports, such as mediation and restorative justice.[5] Likewise, in the US, the American Psychological Association published a report arguing that zero-tolerance policies were not only ineffective but also stood in direct opposition to what was known about child development and best practices in education.[6]

More recently, in 2014, the US Department of Justice and the US Department of Education issued a joint statement that exclusionary discipline was being overused and applied in discriminatory ways. They recommended the use of restorative justice as one of many alternatives to suspensions and expulsions.[7] In the wake of these shifts, there has been a growing awareness and acceptance of RJ in educational contexts. Rather than a teacher here and a school counselor there, recent years have seen entire school districts adopt RJ practices.

Of note has been the work of the Oakland-based RJOY (Restorative Justice for Oakland Youth) in the United States, led by John Kidde, Rita Alfred, and Fania Davis. Drawing on the resources of RJOY, Cole Middle School in West Oakland began initiating RJ training for teachers and other school personnel in 2005 at the prompting of the school's disciplinary case manager. By 2007, RJ had become the primary system for addressing discipline issues at Cole, and students were being trained as circle facilitators. As of 2016, the Oakland district maintains a central RJ office and has an RJ coordinator in almost every middle and high school.

Recent Shifts in RJE

Restorative justice in educational contexts is no longer limited to isolated schools. It is a growing field of its own—connected to the broader RJ community, but with its own practices and principles. Three major shifts can be noted as a result:

1. An expanded understanding of RJE
2. The development of education-specific RJ theory
3. The emergence RJE within teacher preparation programs

First, in the beginning, the application of restorative justice to school-based situations was primarily an attempt to find alternatives to suspensions and expulsions. Most of the early school-based RJ programs focused on student behaviors and on finding ways to address the harm caused by those behaviors. More recently, however, RJ has also been taken up as a way to nurture healthy school climates. The writings of Brenda Morrison and Dorothy Vaandering[8] began to frame students' behavior through a lens of social engagement as opposed to social control, echoing educational research that encouraged shifts in school climate instead of simply trying to change individual student behaviors.

Thus, although some would view restorative justice as a menu of interventions to address harm, many in the educational arena view RJ as a theoretical framework through which to view not only the repairing of harm but also the restoration of healthy relationships, emphasizing just and equitable learning environments. For example, many schools are including a focus on social-emotional learning (SEL) as a part of their restorative justice approaches, recognizing that many students need explicit teaching about how to recognize and respond to emotions.

Second, teachers, counselors, and principals led most of the early restorative justice work in schools. This was a grassroots movement. However, as it has grown, it has become increasingly systematized and built into school structures. Although there was some theory undergirding the early practices, that theory primarily emerged from the disciplines of criminology and sociology—not necessarily from education. There is a need to establish RJE as a field unto itself, albeit as an outgrowth of RJ—one that relies on educational theory integrated with pedagogical considerations.

One of the implications of this growth is the increasing need for resources and research. Some educators have started to write about education-specific RJ theory. For example, in 2004, Belinda Hopkins wrote about whole-school approaches to RJ implementation, asserting that creating *Just Schools* required more than just responses to disciplinary infractions. In 2005, Lorraine Stutzman Amstutz and Judy Mullet wrote *The Little Book of Restorative Discipline for Schools*, laying out foundational principles for applying restorative justice to school-based discipline incidents. In 2007, several books focusing on restorative justice in school contexts were published. Ron and Roxanne Claassen published *Discipline That Restores*, providing a model for school discipline and strategies for creating more respectful and cooperative learning environments. Brenda Morrison wrote the first comprehensive academic account of the development of restorative justice as a response to bullying and school violence in *Restoring Safe School Communities*.

In addition to some of the written resources, there is an increase in the availability of videos and other tools for implementation. A list of resources is included at the end of this book.

Finally, the growth of RJE has led to the inclusion of restorative justice in teacher preparation programs. Previously, most RJ training had either been through professional development or community-based training. Several teacher education programs now offer courses and certificates on restorative justice. For example, the University of Waikato in New Zealand began offering courses in the early 2000s as part of its education program.[9] In 2014, Eastern Mennonite University, located in Harrisonburg, Virginia, USA, initiated the first graduate-level RJE program specifically located in an education department, offering both a master of education with a concentration in RJE and a graduate certificate in RJE.[10] The following year, Simon Fraser University in Vancouver, British Columbia, Canada, followed suit, approving the development of an RJE program in an education department.[11] Because it is important that educational personnel are equipped with the knowledge, skills, and dispositions to lead restorative justice implementation, we believe these types of programs will become more common as RJE continues to grow.

Summary

RJE is growing rapidly. In this chapter, we have situated this growth within a historical context. We acknowledge that it is only a partial history. Our hope is that this history will provide a starting point for others to build on.

One of the primary critiques of restorative justice in education is that it is not easily defined. Although a variety of processes could be identified as restorative, what RJE shares with these processes are fundamental principles and a core set of beliefs and values that guide the work.

This book takes a comprehensive view of RJE, viewing it as a framework, not simply as a set of practices. Within this framework, we see RJE as composed of three overlapping and interdependent components:

1. *Creating just and equitable learning environments*
2. *Nurturing healthy relationships*
3. *Repairing harm and transforming conflict*

In Chapters 4–6, we discuss each of these in greater detail. Before that, however, we take time in Chapter 3 to examine the important role of beliefs and values in RJE.

Chapter 3:
Beliefs and Values in RJE

Think about a decision, big or small, that you made recently and the actions that followed. Now consider which factors influenced your decision:

- Were you influenced by other people?
- Were you influenced by perceptions of the situation?
- Were you influenced by possible consequences?
- Were you influenced by previous experiences?

Because decision making is as much a part of life as breathing, eating, and sleeping, we rarely consider what influences how we make choices. Afterward, we tend to focus on the consequences of a decision. Much like attending only to the flower of a plant, we often forget that growth begins with a seed and depends on roots. Similarly, the seeds and roots of decision making and actions for a person, an organization, an institution, or a society are reflective of beliefs and values.

Restorative justice in education (RJE) has grown from a particular set of beliefs and values. For educators and educational institutions to successfully implement, nurture, and sustain RJE, it is necessary to assess if and how personal and organizational beliefs and values line up with those of RJE. Beliefs and values are often assumed, varied, interconnected, and influenced by our sociocultural contexts. Assessment of these beliefs and values can be difficult, yet positive social change necessitates exploring them.

In this chapter, we adopt another metaphor, the use of eyeglasses, as a way to better recognize our beliefs and values. We further define what we mean by RJE beliefs and values, invite readers to identify personal core beliefs and values, and illustrate how RJE lives out its beliefs and values.

The Glasses That Shape Our View of the World

Howard Zehr, in describing the foundations of restorative justice (RJ), explains that engaging with RJ requires that we examine and change the lenses through which we are seeing the world.[1] Just as properly prescribed eyeglasses help us see things more clearly, so, too, does explicitly articulating our perspectives help us make sense of the world. Our perspectives come from our beliefs and values. Like the frames and lenses of a pair of glasses, beliefs hold values, and values support beliefs. Together they impact our decisions and actions.

27

Beliefs, the frames of our glasses, are specific ideas we accept as true that cannot be fully proven. Although they are often based on experiential evidence or intuition, beliefs also involve feelings of trust and conviction. Beliefs impact our view of the world. Beliefs can include acceptance of things that happened in the distant past (e.g., dinosaurs) or will happen in the future (e.g., climate change), trust in a theory or things unseen (e.g., the big bang theory), faith in supreme beings (e.g., religions), or the conviction of our purpose as people (e.g., individualism). We are introduced to these beliefs from the time we are born, through personal experiences within our families and other sociocultural contexts.

Some of what we believe is rarely questioned. At other times, experiences cause us to confront our beliefs and we decide to accept, adjust, or reject them for new beliefs. Whether they are conscious or unconscious, beliefs shape how we think and act. They become the framework, mind-set, or *perspective* that guides how we live. For example, do we believe that children and youth are miniature adults with a fully developed rational capacity to understand their choices and actions, *or* do we view them as people whose capacity to understand is still developing? In this instance, what we believe about children and youth will influence how we interact with them.

Values, the lenses of the glasses that we look through, represent what we think is important about life. They emerge from our beliefs and can also influence our beliefs. Values come into being through our interactions with others, our environment, and our desire for well-being. As individuals, we know what we need to survive and thrive and will make choices that we believe will nurture our well-being. Returning to the example of how we view children and youth, if we believe them to be miniature adults, we may presume that their actions are intentional and that reprimands and punishment will result in change. Thinking about them as developing people, we presume that their actions indicate they are struggling to handle something difficult and they need support. The first perspective includes values such as obedience, perfection, compliance, and assimilation. The second includes values such as honesty, trust, encouragement, support, relationship, and collaboration.

How do we put on glasses that will allow us to understand RJE? First, we become aware of the fact that we are wearing a particular pair of glasses that shapes how we see the world, and then we see the options available for a different pair. Finally we choose to take off the old and put on the new.

What Glasses Am I Wearing?

What we believe and value might not always be clear. In fact, what we say we believe and value might actually be different from reality. Sometimes beliefs and values are unconscious; other times they are suppressed because they seem to conflict with those of the community. Ultimately, our actions, not our words, most accurately reflect what is at our core. We live up to our beliefs, not to what we say we believe.[2] Deep reflection is needed to bring core beliefs and values to the surface.

One way to do so is to examine our actions. By identifying the values reflected in our actions, we can connect values to core beliefs. Try one or more of these:

- Think of someone in your life you care deeply about. Make a list of what you would miss about that person if you were separated.
- Think of a group of people you engage with through your work or personal life. Make a list of the things you need *from them* to be your best self.
- Find an object that represents *hope* for you. Explain why.

Consider what you have listed. These begin to identify your values. Now choose one value and consider what it indicates about what you believe about people. For example, if you *value affirmation* from others to be your best self, it may point to your *belief* that people are *interconnected* and that we need one another to be fully human.

This is but a beginning experience with a very complex process. Our glasses are also shaped by the social groups we are a part of, such as race, ethnicity, religion, sexuality, gender, ability, class, etc. For example:

- We are both white, middle-class, able-bodied professors with European origins who hold a great deal of privilege. That privilege shapes the glasses we wear, whether or not we like it. When we become aware of our glasses, we can begin to see how our beliefs and values might undermine the well-being of others.

• Many Western societies today are strongly influenced by ideals that elevate individual freedom and free-market economies in pursuit of profit. Educational organizations within these societies typically operate using a corporate model, in which students become commodities, objectified as having value only when they produce high academic standards as defined by test scores.[3]

The complexity involved in identifying beliefs and values can be overwhelming. Simply beginning, however, is important. It will reveal what, if any, distorted views we unwittingly hold. If there is a disconnect between beliefs, values, and actions, don't be discouraged. It's normal and actually better positions us to look for other options. Deep reflection provides the foundation for authentic, sustainable change.

New Glasses

The principles and practices of restorative justice in education are supported by two key beliefs:

• Human beings are *worthy*.
• Human beings are *interconnected* with each other and the world.[4]

Regardless of someone's visible characteristics or actions, that person is of worth simply because he or she is a living, breathing human being. People thrive when they are in good relationships with others and their environments. People are interconnected.

31

> *Respect (re:* again; *spect:* to look): "To look again" from the point of view of the other; to put one's self in the other's shoes and then respond.

Surrounding these beliefs are three core values: respect, dignity, and mutual concern.[5] Respect and dignity speak directly to honoring the worth of people. Mutual concern speaks to our interconnectedness. In considering whether our actions align with these values, we might ask the following questions:

• In my interactions with others and the world, do I give respect by *accepting* them for who they are, or do I want to change them to be more like me or like someone who will meet my needs?
• Do I *treat others with dignity,* engaging fully to highlight the best in them?
• Do I notice what others need to survive and thrive?
• Do I ensure that I am not preventing another person's well-being?

> *Dignity:* Worth that cannot be substituted. People have dignity because the essence of who they are cannot be replaced.

• Do I engage with people to ensure that their well-being is nurtured and that they can flourish?
• Can I see how this supports who I am?

These values encapsulate what it is to be

human from an RJE perspective and therefore, point to the reality that in order to flourish, we need to *belong*. Thus, if externally you are treated as worthy (you are allowed to be connected to others), internally you experience *belonging* (you know what it is to feel secure). From an RJE perspective, we accept that we do not always enact our beliefs and values flawlessly. However, this awareness allows us to address harms without fear, confident that our worth and interconnectedness will be upheld even in tension.

> *Mutual concern:* Much more than a common concern, mutual concern is reciprocal, interconnected caring.

How Do We Put on These Glasses?

At times, we can be myopic, thinking that we personally have a clearer perspective than others have. For example, we might convince ourselves that we do *respect* self, others, and the world we live in. Yet how we define and experience respect may be quite different from how others do so. The variations in who we are as people make living relationally complex. So then, how can we put on the glasses of RJE?

One approach we have found helpful invites us to reflect critically on our own interactions with others by answering three questions:

1. Am I honoring?
2. Am I measuring?
3. What message am I sending?[6]

Am I Honoring?

Honoring people is a way of accepting others for who they are. It requires that I consider whether I am aware of the needs, perspectives, and cultures of others as fully as I am aware of my own. It also requires careful asking and listening, trusting others and dispensing with a desire to "fix" or "help" them. Belonging and support are nurtured when I am willing to be present with another without judging that person.

Am I Measuring?

Measuring people is a way of judging others (or myself) to see if they fit my expectation of who I think they *should* be. Measuring places me in a position of power where my own worth is affirmed by someone else's lack of ability or worth. The perceived inadequacies of the other validate my own worth.

We are encouraged constantly within Western society to measure one another and to form groups that welcome some and marginalize others. For example, commerce creates divisions between those who "have" and those who "have not." Through advertising we are made to feel inferior or superior based on ownership of the latest gadgets and fashions. Schools, in a similar way, are designed to label and group students based on ability and behavior. Comparisons and assessment can be necessary and helpful, but when we do measure, it is important to determine the purpose of measuring. For example, we might ask, "Is my measurement of Sasha's ability to read nurturing her well-being or primarily a way of highlighting my capacity to teach well?"

It can be presumptuous to think we can identify what constitutes someone's well-being. How can I really be sure that my actions are contributing to worthiness and interconnectedness of others? Thus the next question gives others the opportunity to provide feedback about our interaction.

What Message Am I Sending?

This question requires empathy and compassion. Either I empathetically put myself in the other's shoes in an attempt to understand our interaction, or I compassionately ask the other directly whether they considered our engagement honoring. All of our words and actions send messages to the people we are with that assure them of how or if they belong. We won't fully know the messages we are sending unless we ask.

Living with RJE Glasses

Putting on RJE glasses by examining our interactions with others may feel odd at first. As we grow, the three questions remind us of our changing perspectives, and we may find it tiring to continuously be this reflective. Though the view may be clearer, we may find it distinctively different from our regular view. At times, the discrepancy between our new view and what we used to experience is magnified. We may need to take off our new glasses at times because of the discomfort. However, as we experience more authentic relationships, we will find ourselves reaching for them. In time we will no longer be as conscious of our "new" view. Wearing RJE glasses is a relief in that honoring the worth and

35

interconnectedness of all people with respect, dignity, and mutual concern usually resonates with who we are personally.

With an RJE perspective, we come to acknowledge each other's vulnerabilities and contributions. Fear of conflict and difference diminishes. Instead of becoming protective and defensive, we engage with one another to find ways to move forward so that everyone's well-being is nurtured. Ultimately, living with RJE glasses allows us to look at life as an opportunity for social engagement rather than social control.[7]

Summary

This chapter highlights the need to identify and examine personal beliefs and values for resonance with those of RJE. In addition, it is also important to examine how RJE beliefs and values align with the core beliefs and values of educational institutions. Understanding how these resonate or differ from each other will shape how RJE is developed and sustained.

Returning to the analogy of the plant, this chapter explores the seed (beliefs) and the initial roots (values) of RJE. Without them there would be no way to anchor or feed the principles and practices of RJE that are expressed explicitly through creating just and equitable learning environments, nurturing healthy relationships, and repairing harm and transforming conflict.

SECTION 2
Examining the Components of Restorative Justice in Education

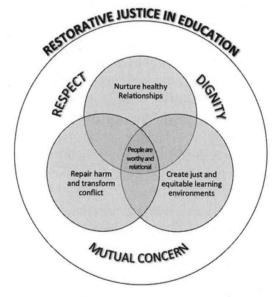

Chapter 3 articulates the central belief that all people are worthy and relational as a foundational tenet of restorative justice in education (RJE), encircled by the key values of respect, dignity, and mutual concern. In Section 2 we move to look at the three core components of RJE.

- Chapter 4 discusses the importance of creating just and equitable learning environments.
- Chapter 5 examines the explicit nurturing of healthy relationships.
- Chapter 6 explains the comprehensive nature of repairing harm and transforming conflict.

As illustrated in the preceding diagram, the three components of RJE not only intersect but also revolve around the same hub of core beliefs and values. Concepts discussed in each of the following three chapters overlap with and inform the others. For example, a key to nurturing healthy relationships is the establishment of just and equitable learning environments *and* an ability to assess power dynamics in relationships to productively address conflict and harm. Intertwined in this way, one is not more important or a prerequisite for another. All of them are essential.

In Section 2, the chapters share a similar three-part structure.

1. We discuss terminology and the importance of the topic for school culture.
2. We explain how RJE informs and engages with each component.
3. We provide concrete actions steps that support educators in implementing the component comprehensively.

These action steps are not exhaustive but are meant to serve as possible starting points for applying the foundational concepts. RJE is dependent on context. As you begin to engage with the concepts and activities in these chapters, more concrete action steps that match the unique needs and gifts of your school community will emerge. Additionally, each chapter contains various "callout boxes" that provide questions, activities, thoughts, or suggestions for consideration. These can be used individually or in groups and are intended to support efforts for making each concept a reality.

Chapter 4:
Creating Just and
Equitable Learning
Environments

Before you begin reading, take a moment to jot down some words or pictures that come to mind when you think about justice and equity. How do you imagine these ideas playing out in school settings? What is educational justice? What is an equitable learning environment? How is justice applied and experienced in your educational context?

Creating just and equitable learning environments is complex. It requires a clear understanding of justice and equity, as well as an awareness of injustice. However, understanding and awareness alone are insufficient. Intentional collaboration, education, and a commitment to the beliefs and values discussed in Chapter 3 are necessary, as are nurturing healthy relationships (Chapter 5) and the ability to address conflict and harm (Chapter 6).

Consider the following scenarios:

- Lisa struggled to sound out the word *categorize* on the state-mandated mathematics exam. As an eighth grader, failing this exam would mean she would have to start her high school math sequence with pre-algebra, which would prevent her from taking the necessary math courses to earn a college prep diploma. She was good in math; she just couldn't read this word.

- Terry just accepted a position as a fifth-grade language arts teacher. He knows that his public school cannot legally discriminate against him based on his sexual orientation, but he fears that if students, parents, or other teachers find out that he is gay, he may face social alienation or increased scrutiny about his performance. As a result, he remains silent and avoids conversations related to his personal life.

- Kali walked into his third-grade classroom on a Monday early in December to find a brightly lit tree, a large picture of Santa Claus on the wall, and Christmas music playing softly in the background. He sighed, feeling slightly out of place, and worried that the other children would find out that his family doesn't celebrate Christmas.

Defining Justice and Equity

Everyday, many children and educators go to school and find themselves in situations where the deck is stacked against them. Some of them feel marginalized based on race, gender, or sexual orientation. Others experience school as disconnected from their lives due to language, religion, social class, or ability. To understand this reality more fully, it is important to grasp the essence of justice and equity.

Justice

Attempts to define the concept of justice are met with significant challenges; the word itself has been used in different ways and has been employed to mean anything from a person who acts as a judge (e.g., chief justice) to a system for enforcing a set of laws (e.g., the criminal justice system) to a way of distributing resources among people (e.g., social justice). As a result of the ways in which the word *justice* has been employed to mean so many things, some opt to use different language when talking about *restorative justice* (RJ).

For example, some restrict the use of the term *restorative justice* to reactive responses to crime and wrongdoing, while others prefer the language of *restorative discipline* to indicate a specific approach to addressing behavioral concerns. Various other terms have been created to indicate more proactive practices designed to build community within and beyond educational settings, such as *restorative approaches* or *restorative practices.*

While we honor the work of those who use other terminology, we hold on to the term *justice* as a way to highlight the comprehensive nature of primary justice in RJE, which is about the reciprocal pursuit of what everyone needs for their individual and collective well-being. It embraces respect, dignity, and mutual concern as a way to honor the worth of all (e.g., they experienced justice). This encompasses much more than secondary justice, which addresses behavior and administering consequences to people who do wrong (e.g., justice was served). It includes examining asymmetrical relationships and finding

43

ways to provide for the needs of everyone in those relationships. These ideas are well grounded in a variety of traditions.

Howard Zehr equates *justice* with the Hebrew word *shalom*. Here, justice is about "right" relationships in which "right" refers to things as they are supposed to be. Relatedly, the Hebrew word *sedeqah* is about "right" living or righteousness. When we seek to live in *shalom, sedeqah* is the act of doing justice. *Sedeqah* does not indicate a passive stance but rather an active, engaged doing of justice. Thus, within the Judeo-Christian tradition, *justice* is about the "positive presence of harmony and wholeness, of health and prosperity, of integration and balance . . . the state of soundness or flourishing in all dimensions of existence."[1]

Islam holds similar ideas about peace and justice. Amir Akrami, a theological scholar from Yale Divinity School, notes that the word *salaam* refers to a sense of peace, health, and wholeness. Incorporating this word into a common greeting, *assalamu alaikum* conveys a desire for peace and wholeness to the recipient of the greeting. The Arabic word *adala* is most closely aligned with the concept of justice and denotes the Quranic concept of "putting things in their right and appropriate place, where they are supposed to be."[2]

Likewise, justice and equity are foundational within indigenous traditions. The medicine wheel in native spirituality, for example, symbolizes balance and harmony. In addition, the word *namwayut* (from the Musqueam people), meaning "we are all one," points us to the importance of living in balance and harmony with one another. When we live

44

namwayut, we acknowledge the interdependence of humanity and work to ensure that relationships are healthy and that reconciliation occurs in ways that are just. The Honorable Chief Justice Dr. Robert Yazzie of the Navajo Nation differentiates between horizontal justice and vertical justice. Within vertical justice, the offender and the victim are seen as separate and detached; the outcomes are defined by winning and losing. Within horizontal justice, equality is like a circle in which no one is more important than another. We are all one. The outcome of justice is related to wholeness and healing rather than right and wrong. Furthermore, helping another person is more important than determining fault. Responsibility lies with each of us to repair harm and restore justice.[3]

> Take a moment and think about the spiritual or moral traditions that ground your understanding of justice, equity, and wholeness. How do the concepts of RJE align with those traditions?

Within these traditions, there is a close connection between the concepts of justice and peace. According to criminologist Elizabeth Elliott, "A peaceful, safe and just society begins with individuals who are at peace with themselves living in peaceful interactions with others."[4] Without a sense of peace, where harmony among all is realized, there isn't really any justice. Conversely, without a sense of justice, peace

45

is difficult to achieve. Ursula Franklin, a physicist and peace activist, defined peace as the absence of fear and suggested that by overcoming oppression, justice creates a world where there is no need to fear another.[5] Thus, for RJE, any attempt at building peace requires that justice be an essential component.

In summary, Carolyn Boyes-Watson and Kay Pranis remind us that justice is not about laws or defined behaviors, but rather about relationships. They argue that human beings have a strong, innate sense of things that are just and equitable. When our relationships are experienced as unjust, we can build up "negative emotions, such as anger, resentment, distrust and humiliation that often motivate people to take action to correct the imbalance or injustice." Conversely, when relationships are viewed as just, we experience "a sense of harmony, peace, stability, and satisfaction."[6]

Equity

Equity means fairness or impartiality. Unlike equality, which suggests that everyone is treated the same or gets the same share, equity focuses on equal outcomes and requires that everyone gets what they need in order to experience well-being. We often assume that in order to be fair, everyone has to be treated the same. That would be fine if we all started from the same place—but we don't.

The crucial difference between equity and equality can be illustrated by looking at zero-tolerance policies in school settings. In the early 1990s, zero-tolerance policies were implemented, claiming to be fairer than preceding disciplinary policies because all students were to be treated exactly the same. For example, in a situation in which two students got into a fistfight, zero-tolerance policies required that both be suspended from school for ten days, regardless of the circumstances. Supposedly, a predetermined consequence would prevent disparities, leveling the playing field for all students.

As research has shown, however, zero-tolerance policies not only failed to make schools safer but actually exacerbated unequal treatment.[7] Despite the rhetoric about treating everyone equally, these policies grossly exacerbated disproportionate (i.e., inequitable) discipline rates for students of color, those coming from economically disadvantaged families, those placed in special education, and LGBTQ students.[8] In attempting to treat everyone the same, schools overlooked factors such as bullying, school failure, trauma, racism, etc., that impacted students' behaviors. By ignoring the needs arising from these injustices, many students weren't actually treated fairly at all. The policies intended to create equality actually led to an objectification of students, as though the incidents leading to disciplinary responses were disconnected from everything else in their life.

Equity, in contrast to equality, asks this question: What do people need in order to experience well-being?

Returning to the zero tolerance example, the two students who got into a fight might have done so for vastly different reasons, representing different needs. Let's imagine that for one student, the fight was due to underlying academic frustration that then erupted in the cafeteria; for the other, the fight was in retaliation for being bullied earlier in the day. Although theoretically treated "equally" in that they were both suspended for ten days, they weren't treated equitably—neither got what he needed. Furthermore, the needs of others who were impacted by the fight—students and staff—were completely ignored.

There is a temptation to assume that because something seems just and fair to us, it should be obviously so for others. The problem with that reasoning is that people's sense of what is just and fair varies. When people say, "That's not fair," it is important to have a respectful dialogue to understand their notion of justice. What is it about their experience that feels unjust for them? We don't have to share their perspective, but if we are going to be effective at addressing their frustration, we must at least try to understand it.

> Let's wrestle with the word *fair* for a minute. When a student complains, "That's not fair," what he likely means is that someone else got something he didn't. He's talking about equality. How might we instead create an environment of equity where well-being, not sameness, is our goal?

In an RJE school, a focus on justice and equity creates space for understanding and for addressing underlying needs that often manifest in undesirable behavior. In the preceding example, a focus on justice and equity would potentially have prevented the fight from happening in the first place. By working to ensure that one student received appropriate academic support while the other had a safe place to address the bullying, needs would have been met prior to behaviors escalating.

In the rest of this chapter, we provide additional examples demonstrating how RJE practices can work to promote just and equitable learning environments.

How RJE Addresses Issues of Justice and Equity

In this section, we discuss three ways that schools implementing RJE might address issues of injustice and inequity. There is a long history of people seeking more just and equitable ways of doing school. For example, the National Council of Teachers of English (NCTE) has recently included an emphasis on social justice and equity in its standards for the preparation of teachers.[9] Resources, such as *Reading, Writing, and Rising Up: Teaching about Social Justice and the Power of the Written Word* by Linda Christensen, focus on teaching social justice to students using content-area curriculum. Publications such as *Rethinking Schools* and *Teaching Tolerance*

> Review the core values of RJE: respect, dignity, and mutual concern. As you read this section, note places where these values are enacted (e.g., relationships, policies, school routines).

provide extensive resources for educators who desire to include more socially just pedagogy in their practices. Resources such as these can support the work of RJE to nurture more just and equitable school environments.

Promoting Just and Equitable Relationships

Because RJE is a relational framework, school-based relationships should be characterized by justice and equity. Restorative justice processes are designed to facilitate relationships in which everyone is treated with worth and dignity, regardless of their race, ethnicity, religion, nationality, ability, economic class, language, body type, gender, or sexual orientation. For example, circle processes allow for everyone in the circle to have an opportunity to speak from their own experience. In the circle, no one is more important than another and everyone's perspectives are respected. Likewise, when harm occurs, restorative conferencing is primarily a space for those harmed to have their needs met; this further ensures upholding the worth and dignity of all. Those causing harm are held accountable and have the opportunity to contribute to the healing process where possible.

Restorative justice practices create spaces to be heard, but part of building a restorative ethos in a school is creating those spaces in less structured ways. According to Kay Pranis, "Justice is not about getting even, but rather about getting well." One way we can help our students experience healing is by listening to them. This is particularly true for students who have often been marginalized or who have experienced school as a harmful place. For all students, but for these students in particular, taking time to meet with them during or after school to hear about what is important in their lives will create a relationship that supports them. This simple act of reaching out has the potential for preempting the meltdown they may have had later in your biology class.

Addressing Underlying Needs

Just and equitable outcomes means working to ensure that people get what they need. According to criminologists Dennis Sullivan and Larry Tifft, "We develop our potentialities as human beings and enhance our collective well-being when our needs are respected, expressed, listened to, defined with care, and ultimately met."[10] One of the core principles of RJE is a commitment to addressing the needs of all of those in the community. Even when those needs cannot be met fully, there is still value in the acknowledgment of those needs.

In addition to the work of Abraham Maslow and Carl Rogers, who led the way in developing theories about human needs, years of educational research have concluded that several "universal" core needs drive motivation:

1. **Autonomy:** a sense of control over our own destiny
2. **Belonging:** the assurance that we are accepted, valued, and respected
3. **A sense of competence:** the assurance that we are capable[11]

Similarly, Howard Zehr articulated three core needs that serve as pillars of RJ and that are fundamental for well-being:

1. **Autonomy:** a sense of personal control and empowerment
2. **Order:** a sense of trust about the world we live in and how it works
3. **Relatedness:** a sense of connection and where we fit in our relationships

Zehr says that when those core needs are not met, "we may construct a world in which we establish a sense of *autonomy* by domination over others, an *order* based on violence and force, and a sense of *relatedness* rooted in distrust of others and kinship with fellow 'outsiders.'"[12] For example, a student who feels that she doesn't have any friends may resort to illicit behavior in order to gain a sense of belonging. Attempts to control the student's behavior may end up exacerbating the problem by taking from her the very control that she is working so diligently to obtain.

RJE is about addressing underlying needs. For example, consider students' need for autonomy. In schools committed to RJE, there is an emphasis on shared decision making and a commitment to *power with* rather than *power over*. (See Chapter 5 for more details). RJE recognizes that people are capable of making good decisions. Sometimes they need guidance, but that should never prevent them from being involved in making decisions about their future, about their behavior and about their academics.

RJE acknowledges the learning needs of students and the importance of instruction that promotes the active engagement of all learners. Drawing on Paulo Freire's work, restorative educators resist the "banking model" of education, in which students are passive recipients of the teacher's knowledge; instead, the prior knowledge and experiences of all learners are considered valuable for learning.[13] Students are taught within their zone of proximal development,[14] and instruction is differentiated according to content, process, product, affect, and environment.[15] Acknowledging that all students bring worth to our classrooms, an RJE framework seeks to address the underlying social, emotional, and academic needs of each student.

Explicitly Addressing Injustices

As many schools become increasingly diverse, there has been an increased awareness of the need to implement culturally responsive pedagogy.[16] Unfortunately, initiatives that promote cultural competence, intercultural teaching, and multicultural education have too often been limited to discussions about foods, dress, and dance. Furthermore, they have been restricted to certain months of the school year or specific aspects of the curriculum. As Paul Gorski and Katy Swalwell warn, too often "diversity initiatives avoid or whitewash serious equity issues."[17]

We can't just talk about welcoming or valuing diversity without acknowledging that many students who fall outside of the dominant majority experience unaddressed discrimination and marginalization daily. For example, as noted earlier, discipline statistics over the past forty years reveal a gross disparity between white students and students of color. Even the most student-centered discipline policies too often focus on helping students become more like the dominant majority and fail to address implicit bias that is often woven into curriculum and school practices. Disparities also show up in enrollment in advanced placement and honors classes; white students are more likely to have access to and enroll in those classes than students of color.[18]

When schools and classrooms perpetuate racial or ethnic discrimination, whether intentional or not, we should expect students to feel disconnected, disengaged, and defiant. RJE prioritizes justice and equity where

- the vulnerable are cared for,
- the marginalized are included,
- the dignity and humanity of each person in the educational setting matters, and
- everyone's needs are heard and met.[19]

In a school where RJE has been embraced, there are concrete action steps that seek to address issues of implicit bias and discrimination.[20]

Concrete Action Steps to Support Just and Equitable Learning Environments

Return to the thinking box at the beginning of this chapter and consider the words and images you equated with justice and equity. Have those images changed after reading this chapter? The images we use to portray justice and equity will impact the types of decisions we make in schools. The desire to create more just and equitable schools must be accompanied by actions. Here are two areas where concrete steps can be taken.

Culturally Inclusive Pedagogy

One way to think about supporting justice and equity is in decisions about curriculum and instruction. As noted earlier, a great number of resources for educators are related to culturally responsive pedagogy.[21] In RJE schools, curricular decisions are made in ways that honor and respect all people regardless of their race, ethnicity, language, gender, sexual orientation, income, or ability. Here are some ideas:

- When choosing textbooks, consider finding authors with diverse backgrounds and who bring a wide range of experiences.
- Ensure that literature for children and youth reflects the diversity of students in the school and features characters who look, talk, and live like them.
- Use resources and materials that consider historical harms and highlight the experiences of those who have been ignored. For example, history classes should not only address the ways in which indigenous peoples were brutalized but also highlight the contributions that they have and continue to make.
- Poetry and literature units should include writings from more than just white European authors.

Beyond materials and resources, the classroom environment also creates opportunities for promoting justice and equity. At times, teachers and administrators can overlook the gaps that exist between their own experiences and those of their students. Consider the following:

- Think about the *sample problems* used in math and science classes. Are they relevant to the lived experiences of all of our students, or do they make assumptions based on majority views? One science teacher intentionally references breakthroughs made by women in STEM (science, technology, engineering, and math) fields in order to promote gender equity.
- Think about the *words we use.* How easily teachers can perpetuate assumptions about marriage and relationships without considering that some children live with aunts or uncles, two moms, or foster parents. One teacher in Virginia refers to students' "grown-ups" rather than their parents in an effort to be more inclusive about possible family configurations.
- Think about *equity issues* related to religious diversity. If you celebrate the religious holidays of one group of students, then the holidays of all students should be celebrated. Putting up a Christmas tree and singing Christmas carols is appropriate, as long as other students, like Kali at the beginning of this chapter, are also invited to share and have their holiday traditions honored. In an RJE classroom, for example, the third-grade teacher might also have other winter celebrations represented in the class decorations, or students might sit in a circle together and share stories with the class about their various holiday traditions.

Full Participation for All Members of the Community

Another way to consider justice and equity in schools and classrooms is to ensure that all members of the community can participate fully in school-related events and activities. Students who feel marginalized are often disconnected from learning and from social interaction. They are often underrepresented in advanced placement classes, overrepresented in remedial classes, less likely to be recognized for their accomplishments, and more likely to drop out of school. One concrete thing schools can do is complete an internal equity audit and then make policy decisions that promote justice and equity.

One way that RJE promotes full participation is with students requiring special education services. Research suggests that students with special needs are suspended or expelled at disproportionately higher rates than non-identified students. To counter this, special educators like Leila Peterson[22] and Julie Camerata[23] are working to blend

Many RJE practitioners, such as Anita Wadhwa of the Restorative Justice Collaborative of Houston, are equipping students to facilitate circle processes. How might you work to ensure that students are more involved in the RJE work at your school?

RJE and special education in ways that reduce exclusionary discipline for students with special needs and that ensure that their instructional needs are fully met. In addition, Peterson and Camerata promote full participation by creating spaces where students receiving special education services are invited to participate in their annual IEP (individualized education program) meetings and to give input on instructional decisions.[24]

Within RJE, equitable participation is not limited to students. When meetings occur, all who have a stake in the decisions being made should be invited so that their voices are heard. For example, invite cafeteria and custodial staff to give input on school-related decisions. Include teachers in decisions about curriculum and instruction. Place a priority on the involvement of parents, caregivers, and family members of students as essential members of the learning community.

Summary

RJE leads us to focus on the worth, well-being, and relational essence of being human. There is a deliberate shift away from individualism toward interconnectedness, treating one another with justice and equity.

Chapter 5:
Nurturing Healthy
Relationships

Take 3–5 minutes to draw a mind map of the relationships you encounter and impact in one day; you can use pictures and/or words. Begin by putting yourself in the center of the page. From here, make a web that identifies each of the people you have direct contact with in a regular school day. Next, add the names of all the places where you work and live. Finally, add a word or two to each of these that describe your feelings when you are relating with these people and places.

The quantity, complexity, and reach of relationships that occur in a school are mind-boggling. When educators' beliefs and values align with those of restorative justice in education (RJE), relationships become evident wherever we look, as does the realization that their quality shapes the school's culture and students' ability to learn. Thus, nurturing healthy relationships is an essential element for just and equitable learning environments, as well as for addressing harm and conflict.

Three stories illustrate the comprehensiveness of relationships and how they are nurtured—from the interpersonal to the social, from the more obvious to the subtle:

- Anxiety overwhelms Alys each time she enters the staffroom when Clare is there. She feels inadequate as Clare continues to make comments about Alys's overly boisterous students. Using the principles of RJE that she encourages her students to use, Alys summons the courage to have a conversation with Clare. It was not an easy conversation, but it was helpful. Through the experience, Alys is reminded how conversations can become supportive or adversarial through the nuances of dialogue.
- Ken is struck by the messages inherent in the math curriculum. Eager for his students to understand the world of finance for personal and social well-being, he reads the problem-solving activities and discovers a repeated emphasis on the "buying power" of the individual with little regard for addressing the concerns of people marginalized by poverty. He begins to revise the learning activities to honor the worth and interconnectedness of all people.
- Trevor goes to the office to pick up a late slip before going to his first-grade class. He stands on his tiptoes to ring the bell on the counter. He waits quietly until he hears a voice asking him what he needs. After he leaves, Ms. Cortes wonders how she would feel if she were Trevor. She is glad that

60

plans are being made to redesign the office spaces to be more child-friendly.

The Challenge of the Current Context

Our ability to nurture and maintain healthy relationships is often assumed—much like breathing. However, in Western societies where individuals are often disconnected from their communities, "breathing" is becoming labored, painful, and shallow because the inherent need to belong has been undermined. The results include growing levels of anxiety and other diagnoses of mental illness, escalating interpersonal and social conflicts, high student and educator dropout rates, and ongoing school suspensions and expulsions. Educators are noting and struggling to respond to increasing needs, and recent research identifies diagnoses of toxic stress for growing numbers of children and youth from all sociocultural contexts who struggle to bond and build trust with parents, teachers, and/or guardians. These caregivers, often in spite of good intentions, are themselves disconnected and preoccupied, caught in hectic lifestyles without the knowledge or means for meeting the needs of their children.[1]

RJE is a significant response to a disconnected society. Healthy relationships, characterized by attachment and belonging, are a critical element for well-being. RJE uniquely emphasizes people's *dependence* on one another, not their independence. For relationships to become mutually beneficial, or *interdependent*, it is necessary to be aware of what constitutes quality relationships.

Identifying Quality Relationships

Healthy relationships are nurtured when people communicate respectfully and share power in a way that allows for individual and collective needs to be met. Respectful communication occurs when people take into account the reality that the messages they send and receive will have an impact on others' sense of worth and well-being. It encourages people to be at their best even in challenging circumstances. This is possible when people recognize the role power plays. Inherently, power is neither good nor bad. How power is used will impact the health of relationships.[2] When power is employed in self-serving ways, relationships are diminished because others are used as objects to further the well-being or success of self. The questions introduced in Chapter 3—*Am I measuring? Am I honoring? What message am I sending?*—help uncover the impact of power in relationship. If I measure others, I send messages that there is an imbalance of power and one of us has *power over* the other. If I honor others, I send messages that I am willing to share *power with* you. If I consciously consider what messages I send when I communicate, I am alert to the possibility of power imbalance.

Educational institutions have been designed to be hierarchical. People in schools often experience or engage with power in unbalanced ways. When people feel they are required to submit to another's power, it is common for them to push back and exert their own power either subtly or overtly. They might also simply comply with the stronger power and negate their own worth. Because every action results in interaction, RJE works to ensure that power is

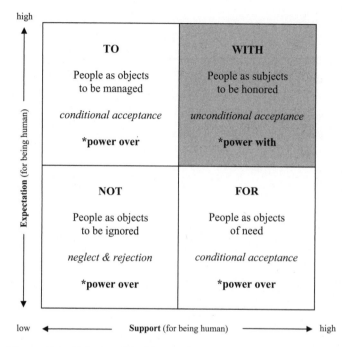

Expectation (for being human)

TO	WITH
People as objects to be managed	People as subjects to be honored
conditional acceptance	*unconditional acceptance*
*power over	***power with**
NOT	FOR
People as objects to be ignored	People as objects of need
neglect & rejection	*conditional acceptance*
*power over	***power over**

low ◄─────── **Support** (for being human) ────────► high

Figure 5.1: Relationship Matrix (power over; power with).

employed in a manner that nurtures well-being. The Relationship Matrix[3] (Figure 5.1) illustrates this.

Power is embodied in the *support* and *expectations* that people have for one another's humanity (their worth and interconnectedness) as identified in the horizontal and vertical axes. When people provide support and expectations in a balanced, reciprocal way, power is used constructively, is available to all involved, and results in people engaging *with* each other. However, power becomes destructive in relationships if one sees it as a limited and desirable commodity. Because everyone needs to belong, doing what is necessary to belong then becomes

competitive. Those who feel powerless will do whatever necessary to gain control, find acceptance, or
retreat, while those in power will do whatever necessary to maintain their position. In either situation,
power-over relationships result in people doing things
to or *for* each other, or more profoundly, ignoring
each other completely (*not*).

The Relationship Matrix helps identify how we are
in relationship with others. When relationships are
new or become conflicted, the matrix can reveal gaps
in support or expectations. Using it to assess strong
relationships can reveal how support and expectations can be provided in balanced ways. When
relationships are unbalanced, people become objects
for the benefit of others. When they are balanced,
relationships radiate respect, dignity, and mutual
concern for each other.

Applying the Relationship Matrix

How can the Relationship Matrix be applied?
Consider the following examples:

- *WITH:* Chris, a fourth-grade teacher, recognizes
  that she is in a position of power as an educator and
  that she could be using power to diminish or nurture the worth of a student, colleague, or parent.
  As a teacher engaged in RJE, she aims to provide
  high support and high expectations. She works *with*
  her students so teaching and learning is reciprocal.
  When her class is repeatedly off-task on an assignment and she is unable to identify why, she calls
  her students to a talking circle meeting (described
  later) where each one is invited to respond to this

question: "What is happening that makes it difficult to focus?" They share that the current assignment is too similar to one done in a previous grade. Chris is impressed with their ideas when she asks, "What should we do about this?" Then together they make a plan and adapt the unit. By *honoring* them as growing human beings and responding to their circumstances, Chris holds them accountable to their responsibility in a supportive, collaborative manner. She does not attempt to control but instead engages them.

- *TO:* Chris also knows what it feels like to do things *to* her students and is uncomfortable with those memories. During the previous week, she kept two students in at recess to complete their work and then went to the staffroom for coffee. She was too tired and frustrated to ask them what was happening that they couldn't finish their assignment in the time allotted. She also recalls the rewards charts that she publicly put stickers on for students working productively, embarrassing those students who were struggling to keep up. In both cases, her expectations exceeded her willingness to provide support. She is often tempted to use *power over* students to control their actions. When her students conform, it makes her look good. Teaching would be so much easier if the students were robots who did what they were programmed to do!

- *FOR:* Chris also recalls times when she provided high support but set low expectations for students. Because parents in prominent jobs intimidated her, she catered to the needs of their children. When they came late regularly or didn't contribute in class, she used her power to do things *for* them. She accepted their excuses readily, worked with them until they were done with their work, and communicated in a friendly manner with them. Chris knows now that she tried to be their friend and was using them for her benefit. When she is honest with herself, she admits far less patience for students in foster care or with parents on social assistance.

- *NOT:* Chris also knows what it is to *not* engage with her students. One year she was exhausted and burned out. It took all her energy just to show up for work. She has little memory of those students and realizes that she provided very little support or expectations for them. She created activities that were overly simple so she could sit at her desk while they worked. She was in survival mode and really needed help herself.

Chris's experience illustrates how it is possible for one person to engage with all four of the quadrants depending on the circumstances. Though the descriptions are straightforward to demonstrate the process of critical reflection, the reality often feels more complex. Sharing power in a balanced way can be difficult because relationships are always changing. The resulting growth, however, is beautiful as illustrated in the first

> Think of times when you have engaged in relationships that would fit each of the four quadrants. What do you notice?

example, where Chris shared *power with* the students who gained self-confidence. They realized that their perspectives were important!

How RJE Understands and Supports Healthy Relationships in Education

RJE is primarily a means for changing self, not a means for changing others.[4] This separates RJE from programs and approaches that have changing the behavior of children and youth as their goal. The focus on self may be surprising if educators believe that changing behavior is a key task for education. However, stemming from the belief that people are worthy and interconnected, restorative educators do not manage or control their students, but they become facilitators who create space and opportunities where students can engage. In this way, RJE creates invitational opportunities in which engagement, rather than control, is encouraged.

Recognizing that change begins with self, Ripples of Relationship (Figure 5.2)[5] illustrate the scope of an

Listen for the phrases *classroom management, classroom control,* or *behavior management* in your particular context. Ask the following: What is the intention of this terminology? Does it encourage you to *engage* with your students or *control* them?

educator's interconnectedness in the school context. RJE begins with adults living in supportive relationships that create cultures where everyone—including children, youth, and other vulnerable populations—are honored as worthy, contributing members. Similar diagrams could be created from the point of view of students, caregivers, other support personnel, or broader community members.

Ripples of Relationship begin with a pebble thrown into water. All of our relationships are impacted by our conscious or unconscious beliefs and values. These are stable until our interactions with self and others disrupt our well-being or the well-being of

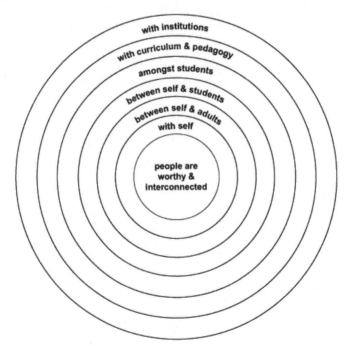

Figure 5.2: Ripples of Relationship

others. When disruption happens, we often rethink or recommit to what we believe and value. Thus, the ripples reverberate outward from the center, but they can also be reversed as various encounters occur. We are individuals within a relational context where we impact and are impacted by those around us.

Out of core beliefs and values, our relationship *with self* is impacted—a relationship that is often ignored or assumed. When we know ourselves well, our responses to others are more likely to be guided by a balance of support and expectations. Positive self-esteem and self-image are crucial. Yet when they are encouraged apart from a belief that all are worthy and relational, individualism and narcissism can result and undermine meaningful relationships. RJE affirms that in order to nurture interconnectedness, we need to see ourselves as valued, contributing parts of relationships. For some of us, it is easier to be self-deprecating

"A person with Ubuntu is open and available to others, affirming of others, does not feel threatened that others are able and good, for he or she has a proper self-assurance that comes from knowing that he or she belongs in a greater whole and is diminished when others are humiliated or diminished . . ."

—Desmond Tutu, 1999

than self-appreciating for various reasons. When this happens, our interactions with others are negatively impacted. We might refrain from contributing actively, contribute in a way that undermines others, or contribute to boost our own egos. Similar concerns arise when we value ourselves more than others.

Next, our relationships *with adults* are identified. School climates are heavily influenced by how adults relate to each other. If we can engage with our peers and colleagues authentically, we model for children and youth respect, dignity, and mutual concern. However, because of our innate need to belong, it can be difficult to support and encourage accountability for our peers if we fear rejection. It takes courage, confidence, and skill to address difficulty, as avoidance might be easier.

> What happens to the respect offered to substitute teachers when they are called "guest teachers" instead? What happens when you take a moment to ask the custodian how they are?

If we relate well with peers and ourselves, we will more likely engage well *with students*. Because we are in authoritative, guiding roles with children and youth, (i.e., "bigger" than them), it is easy to slip into using *power over* them. By engaging *with* them with the same level of respect, dignity, and mutual concern we have for self and adults, we enter into relationships where we seek their well-being first.

As educators, we can be most effective in supporting students in their relationships with their peers and other adults when our relationships are healthy. Looking at *relationships amongst students,* as authority figures it is easy to slip into thinking that we can identify their issues and "fix it" for them. When we recognize our own shortcomings and realize how challenging our own interactions can be, we are more likely to walk *with* our students in their relationships, listening carefully so we can support them and encourage accountability.

As our awareness of relationships increases, we pay closer attention to the messages we send through *the curriculum content and pedagogy.* We realize that who or what we include or omit in terms of content has serious implications for students' perceptions of others. Curriculum and pedagogy will shape how students learn to relate to each other and their communities.

Finally, our *relationship with the institution* is also impacted. The physical entity, the governing structures, the policies, and the procedures of a school have all been put in place and administered by groups of adults with a common goal. Sometimes that goal was well-meaning; other times the goal was motivated by an intentional desire to control (e.g., colonialism, white supremacy, segregation). Over time, even when the visions, missions, and mandates of institutions intend to share power, they can become vague or distorted. Hierarchical power dynamics are then more likely to take over and control rather than engage their constituents.

Regardless of our roles in a school, as adults we recognize that we can contribute positively or negatively to how the school functions by remembering that bureaucracies are created by people. If they are found to be lacking in any way, people are needed to change them. It is easy to measure and blame "the system" when things go wrong. However, when we are engaged with "the system," we can honor it by advocating for change so the well-being of all becomes central.

Ripples of Relationship (Figure 5.2) identify the range of relationships that exist in educational contexts. Though each is presented as separate, in its own ring, the reality is much more complex as the relationships intersect, overlap, grow, and change, constantly influencing one another. By presenting school culture as a series of ripples, RJE emphasizes the need for a clear understanding of how school relationships are nurtured.

Concrete Action Steps for Nurturing Healthy Relationships

In order to nurture healthy relationships, RJE draws on comprehensive resources available and grounded in other theories (e.g., care theory, social-emotional learning [SEL], learning ecologies, etc.). However, any approach, RJE included, can cause further harm when those involved are unaware of their personal core beliefs and values, or of those of the approach being used. The language of relationships can be prominent, but authentic relationships are easily co-opted by institutional expectations or self-interest. Thus, the first action step for nurturing healthy relationships has been the focus of this book—the awareness, acceptance, articulation, and enacting of core beliefs and values that uphold the interconnectedness, worth, and well-being of all.

Building on an analysis of core beliefs and values, two approaches—talking circles and learning to listen/learning to ask—are particularly relevant for encouraging the growth of relational school cultures. We hope that these approaches will open the way for recognizing the myriad other ways that healthy relationships can be encouraged.

Talking Circles

Talking circles, originating from indigenous cultures, are intentional spaces where the core beliefs and values of RJE are practiced, experienced, and embodied.

Physically, a group sits in a circle and, with the guidance of a facilitator or "circle keeper," discusses agreed-upon topics in a manner where each person is given an opportunity to share. An object of meaning for the group (e.g., a stone, a plant, a stuffed toy, etc.), usually referred to as a "talking piece," is passed from person to person around the circle to indicate who holds the space. People are invited to share, pass, or hold a time of silence when the piece comes to them. The circle, which has no beginning or end, symbolically illustrates that all present are valued as significant and that insights shared are held respectfully within that space.

A facilitator or circle keeper's roles can include inviting people to attend, setting up the space, opening the time, introducing dialogue guidelines, presenting the topic, keeping the conversation focused, and closing the circle.

Though the process appears to be simple and is actually simple enough for even young children to facilitate for their peers, it is also intricately complex. Carolyn Boyes-Watson and Kay Pranis articulate how circle dialogues are much more than just putting chairs in a circle: "We are practicing basic ways that are fundamental to being successful together."[7] Within a circle, individual and collective ideas and needs are brought into one space. By giving people a designated opportunity to hear and be heard, trust develops. Over time, this trust and practice in listening and speaking transfers to relationships away from the circle, positively impacting the ways people relate to one another.

In a school setting, talking circles can take on various formats:

- Talking circles can be very quick, short, and lighthearted as a way of getting to know more about each other and acknowledging each other's presence (e.g., staff meetings, classroom meetings, committee meetings).
- Talking circles can provide time for adults to contribute perspectives about their responsibilities at a meeting or for students to contribute ideas about academic work or social concerns.
- Talking circles can be held at the end of a meeting, a lesson, a day, or a week when everyone shares a question they are left with, one thing they have learned, or something they will do before the next gathering.

- Talking circles can be classroom meetings that provide an opportunity for everyone to contribute to how they experienced the past week and what they need for the coming week.
- Talking circles can explore in-depth curricular topics such as race, privilege, or climate change.
- Talking circles can be spaces to process grief when a peer or colleague dies.
- Talking circles can provide opportunities to address serious harm caused between individuals or the group as a whole.
- Talking circles can be used to gather information for individualized education programs (IEPs) so all contributors with insight into a student's needs have a clear voice (this can also include the student).

A growing variety of resources are available to support learning how to facilitate talking circles (see page 111). However, in-person professional development will help you grasp the nuances involved. It's important to note that facilitating for serious harm is challenging and requires significant training and support. Be aware that further harm can be done if facilitated without proper preparation.

In essence, when talking circles become a key form of communication in classrooms and schools, the culture becomes one in which all are honored as worthy and interconnected.

Learning to Listen and Learning to Ask

To communicate effectively, knowing what we "should" do is not enough. It takes practice to learn *how* to listen for understanding, rather than for replying, and *how* to ask open-ended questions that generate authentic dialogue. Open-ended questions can help critically reflect on what is happening around us. Five key questions suggested in a variety of restorative justice (RJ) literature include the following:

- *What happened/is happening?*
- *What was/am I feeling/thinking?*
- *What is the hardest/best thing for me?*
- *Who is impacted by this? How?*
- *What do I need [to do] to move forward?*

Reflect on how you feel when someone asks you *why* you did something. *Why* often puts people on the defensive and shuts down communication. Observe what happens when you stop asking your students or colleagues "Why?" and instead ask, "What happened?"

These questions can deepen learning, address challenging situations, or be used to explore harmful situations. The responses to these questions tell a story of past, present, and future. In a group context, hearing the responses of others highlights the importance of different perspectives. On our own, the questions encourage us to dig below the obvious.

Three examples illustrate how the questions can be used in very different contexts:

- During a math lesson on probability, Mr. Blake uses a checkup circle. He gathers small groups for five minutes and invites students to respond to one or more of the five key questions. Mr. Blake notices that the students who grasp the concepts share the steps of how they got their answers and then stretch their thinking into life applications. He notices that students who are more uncertain or confused articulate where they are stuck. Some identify the spot where they require support from others. He notices how the lesson becomes relational as the students engage with one another's thinking instead of relying on his expertise or the need for a right or wrong answer.

- As Ms. Slade begins to plan for a new unit, she finds herself confused and overwhelmed by the task. She stops and takes five minutes to go for a walk. As she walks, she talks aloud to herself and answers the key questions. By the time she returns, she realizes that she is unclear about the purpose of the unit and feels that her students with learning challenges will be lost. She digs into the curriculum documents for more detail and then stops to talk to her colleague who had taught this class the previous year. Before she heads home, a plan forward is taking shape.

- Ms. Polet used to struggle to engage in light conversation with students. Now she finds herself approaching students readily, beginning conversations with a light, "What's happening for you today?" or "What's the best thing about the day so far?" She is always struck by how students open up, which allows her to share about her day or ask further about what they are thinking/feeling.

Learning to listen and to ask questions is critical for nurturing relationships. Listening carefully will guide how and what we ask, and how or what we ask will guide our listening. The dialogue that results opens up opportunities for us to turn core beliefs and values into practice.

Summary

Nurturing healthy relationships is a key component of restorative justice in education. When combined with just and equitable learning environments, the setting is well prepared to address situations in which people are in conflict or cause each other significant harm. In Chapter 6 we discuss repairing harm and transforming conflict.

Chapter 6:
Repairing Harm and
Transforming Conflict

Think about a time when you experienced harm.
In that moment, what did you need from others?
List some ideas. Now think about a time when you
caused someone else harm. In that moment, what
did you need from others? List some ideas. Look
at your lists. What do you notice? Are you meeting
these needs for your students? Your colleagues?
Yourself?

Given the primacy of relationships for restorative
justice in education (RJE) initiatives in schools,
it is crucial that we nurture those relationships and
work toward healing when they are compromised.
Our best intentions and efforts at nurturing healthy
relationships can still result in conflict and harm.
That harm leaves us with unmet needs—for repair,
for hope, for autonomy, for belonging. We are able to
nurture our relationships in healthy ways when we
consider what we need and what others need when
relationships break down.

Consider the following situations:

- Jolee sat in the bathroom and stared at the mirror, wishing that she could make herself look more like the other girls in her class. Tears streamed down her face as she recalled their unkind words, relentless and harsh. They teased her all the time and no one, not even her teacher, ever stopped them. It seemed that there was no one who would stick up for her and no one to turn to for help.
- Braden had been in in-school suspension (ISS) for forty-eight days this school year. Most were due to office referrals from his science teacher, Mr. Marks. Braden felt that Mr. Marks seemed to look for ways to get him in trouble. Braden didn't understand why Mr. Marks hated him so much and why everything he did in Mr. Marks's class was wrong.
- Mr. Marks worked tirelessly to provide engaging instructional activities for his students. Most seemed to appreciate the effort and occasionally expressed gratitude for being such a caring teacher. Braden, however, was different. Mr. Marks felt that Braden seldom participated and seemed to look for ways to get out of doing any work. Mr. Marks didn't understand why Braden hated him so much and why he refused to engage with science.

The preceding vignettes highlight the complicated nature of relationships and invite us to think about what is needed in each situation for healing and transformation to occur.

Defining Harm and Conflict

Harm is more than a physical or emotional injury. It is anything that undermines a person's dignity or minimizes their worth. Harm doesn't have to be intentional. We might cause harm with what we deem to be innocent comments or actions.

Likewise, *conflict* is more than simply two people disagreeing. Conflict is a relational interaction. When we engage in conflict, we acknowledge that relationship. We might disagree with someone, but if we don't acknowledge a relationship with the person (i.e., we don't share a mutual concern for one another), it remains a disagreement but not necessarily a conflict. Conflict emerges within relationships when the disagreement has potential implications for the relationship.

The examples of Braden and Mr. Marks illustrate the possibility that both the teacher and the student are experiencing harm. Every time Braden is sent to ISS, it confirms his belief that Mr. Marks is out to get him. It feels like a personal attack on his dignity, perpetuating his sense of injustice and decreasing the likelihood that he will be engaged in science class. Conversely, every time Braden disengages in class, it sends a message to Mr. Marks that Braden doesn't care about learning science. The teacher might take it personally, perceiving it as an attack on his dignity.

Students and teachers alike may go to great extremes to protect their sense of dignity and avoid feeling harmed by the other. Students may lash out at teachers or avoid going to class. Teachers may ignore students or work harder to find ways to exclude them through suspension or expulsion. What if these cycles could be transformed into relationships of mutual concern?

A Word about School Discipline and Student Behavior

This chapter is about harm and conflict, not about student behavior. Even within RJE approaches, too often the focus is limited to "fixing" student behavior while ignoring the context from which that behavior emerges. Think about the image we began the book with: when a flower is not blooming in a garden, we don't automatically blame the flower. For example, we see a student lash out at a teacher with angry words or disrespect and we name that *misbehavior.* Defining it as *misbehavior* allows us to consider the action apart from its context. From an RJE perspective, angry words or disrespect are externalized *responses.* Behavior comes from some place—it has a context. It's possible that the student is academically frustrated and feels embarrassed about her lack of ability. It could be that the teacher inadvertently said something that the student felt was insulting. The possibilities are endless. RJE assumes that there are reasons for students' responses and intentionally creates spaces to uncover those reasons. Simply addressing student behavior without addressing the context will ultimately fail.

RJE moves the focus beyond incidents to the context. The incident is important because it opens doors for us to consider the health of the context, but if all we do is address the incident, we aren't truly addressing harm.

Several great books about addressing school discipline through a contextual lens have been written. For example, *The Little Book of Restorative Discipline for Schools,* by Lorraine Stutzman Amstutz and Judy

Mullet, provides a thorough treatment of restorative discipline as an alternative to punitive approaches for addressing student behavior, while concurrently acknowledging the importance of changing school culture. (For additional resources, see page 111.)

Understanding Harm

In contrast to the current legal system, restorative justice (RJ) defines crime and conflict as a "violation of people and relationships" rather than a violation of rules or laws. RJ seeks to ask a different set of questions. Rather than who broke a rule and what punishments does the person deserve, RJ asks who was harmed, what needs are present because of the harm, and who is obligated to meet those needs.[1]

In schools and classrooms, we too often overlook harms that are not explicitly written in the discipline codes. For example, consider Zach's experience in school. Due to thick glasses that enable him to read better, Zach had been teased since he started middle school. When he decided that he'd had enough and pushed another student, he was suspended for five days for violating the discipline code. But isn't the teasing he had received also a "violation of people and relationships"? Shouldn't it be considered a form of harm? In an RJE setting, the harms, needs, and obligations of each person engaged in the situation would be addressed, creating a more just outcome for all involved.

Harm also extends beyond interpersonal relationships. For example, Billy has difficulty reading, but due to restrictions about the number of students who can be served in special education, he does not qualify. Each day, he enters school without a strong enough foundation in reading to be able to access the curriculum. One day, his history teacher, Mr. Omari, becomes frustrated with him for not being able to complete assignments independently. Sensing Mr. Omari's frustration, Billy yells at him, is sent to the office, and ultimately is suspended for three days. In this situation, who experienced harm? Whose dignity was violated? Who is responsible for creating harm? What responsibility does the system hold for causing harm? How does this incident highlight structural injustices that need to be addressed?

> We have all experienced harm at the hands of "the system." Think about a time when the source of your own pain wasn't a person but something more structural.

What harm do other systemic policies—such as an excessive reliance on standardized testing, English-only immersion policies for English Language Learners (ELLs), and zero-tolerance policies—cause to teachers, students, and families?

As we discuss in Chapter 2, the early 1990s brought about zero-tolerance policies that served to impose mandatory suspensions for specific behaviors. Not only are zero-tolerance policies ineffective, but in many cases they also actually perpetuate the behaviors they are intending to stop because they further harm the one suspended. Students who are excluded from school fall behind academically. They are often labeled or treated with less respect. Feelings of injustice serve to deepen students' loss of dignity, often increasing their defiance toward authority figures.

Citing Carol Gilligan, Howard Zehr notes that those who are considered "offenders" are often those who have experienced injustice. Their behaviors can be seen as an attempt to correct injustice. We are not attempting to excuse their behaviors; rather, we want to understand "what happened" to influence their choices. Unless we address underlying injustices— providing opportunities for them to be included in an RJ process, for example—we may end up reinforcing their sense of injustice. According to Ronnie Casella, some students are able to "bounce back from a suspension or expulsion," but students "who are already negatively affected by poverty, racism, academic failure, and other realities" experience such punishment differently—they often struggle to recover.[2] In a report on the impact of zero-tolerance policies, the American Psychological Association concluded that these policies fail to make schools safer and run "counter to our best knowledge of child development."[3] Sometimes our policies can cause harm.

Trauma, stress, and poverty can also create cycles of harm in school settings that lead to decreased feelings of safety and security, impacting learning, relationships, and the school climate. For example, according to research on adverse childhood experiences (ACEs),[4] students who experience high ACE scores often miss a great deal of school, have trouble maintaining focus, and exhibit impulsive behaviors.

> In what ways has trauma impacted your own life? Take some time to read up on trauma and consider ways your school might create a more trauma-informed school culture.

Violent and defiant behaviors are symptoms of trauma and other injustices. In *The Little Book of Trauma Healing,* Carolyn Yoder notes that the impact of trauma can range from *acting-in* behaviors, such as substance abuse or suicide, to *acting-out* behaviors, such as aggressive behaviors or high-risk activities. Other signs of trauma include apathy, lack of empathy, or impaired communication.[5] Research is emerging that suggests that the effects of historical trauma (e.g., residential schools, slavery, genocide) can be passed along genetically to future generations.[6]

The good news is that research also indicates that the negative impact of trauma can be offset by the care and support of a significant adult. When we create caring places where students' needs are met, there is hope for the restoration of relationships as well as the restoration of dignity, a sense of self, and resiliency. In Walla Walla, Washington, for example, Lincoln High School recognized the impact that trauma, conflict, and stress were having on students. The school implemented a trauma-informed approach with dramatic results. There were fewer office referrals and suspensions. There were also fewer fights, an increase in the graduation rate, an increase in test scores, and an increase in college acceptance among graduates.[7]

Understanding Conflict

Like harm, much has been written about conflict in educational settings. The fields of conflict resolution education and peer mediation have helped transform many conflicts. RJE provides another dimension. Schools that adopt RJE should consider the role that dignity plays in nurturing healthy relationships. The goal is to work with conflict in ways that strengthen an individual's sense of dignity.

Conflict is inevitable within any relationship where there is a sense of mutual concern for another. When conflict emerges, the tendency is to seek a resolution. Professional development for conflict management or conflict resolution in schools is important. Many students (and arguably, many educators) are not equipped with the skills to work through conflict in ways that create peaceable outcomes.

Try this exercise: Think about an incident where there was conflict. Who were the people involved in

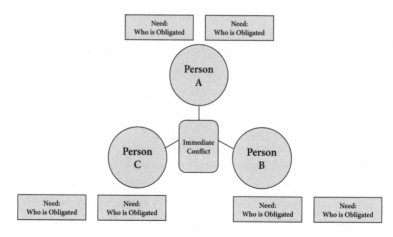

Figure 6.1: Conflict Exercise

that incident? Who experienced harm? Create a diagram like the one in Figure 6.1. Include a circle for each person impacted by the conflict. Then out from each circle, consider what needs are represented by the harm they have experienced. Beside each need, identify who might be able or obligated to meet that need. This type of analysis begins to help us see that conflict is complex and relational.

The way people respond to conflict can either strengthen or harm relationships. Positive outcomes of conflict depend on whether we are able to maintain our dignity in the midst of the conflict. As noted in Chapter 3, dignity is related to our sense of worth. According to Donna Hicks, an international affairs facilitator, our sense of dignity can be disrupted when we are in conflict, leaving us feeling vulnerable, out of control, or worthless. By creating spaces for addressing conflict in ways that restore dignity, we not only resolve the conflict but also potentially transform it into something healing. Conflict, in and of itself, is not detrimental to relationships; conflict that disrupts our sense of dignity is.[8]

Hicks differentiates between dignity and respect. Dignity, she states, is a birthright, inherent in our humanity. We might talk about someone needing to earn respect, but dignity cannot and does not have to be earned; it just is. As with trauma, when our dignity is threatened, we can become irrational in our attempts at survival and self-preservation. This can often lead us to retreat from a situation or to lash out at the threat, creating a cycle of harm. We often see these responses in students (and teachers) who experience conflict as an attack on their dignity.

Dignity is about value, honor, and worth. When we treat others with dignity, we recognize their humanity. That, in and of itself, can be healing for some. When we are treated with dignity, we are able to connect with others in healthy ways, thrive in our academic settings, and talk rationally about conflicts—leading to better outcomes. In the next section, we discuss ways that RJE specifically addresses issues of harm and conflict.

How RJE Addresses Harm and Conflict

Howard Zehr defines RJ as "a process to involve, to the extent possible, those who have a stake in a specific offense and to collectively identify and address harms, needs, and obligations, in order to heal and put things as right as possible."[9] Acknowledging the importance of providing a "guide to how we live together day by day" in schools, Lorraine Stutzman Amstutz and Judy Mullet add this definition:

> [RJ] promotes values and principles that use inclusive, collaborative approaches for being in community. These approaches validate the experiences and needs of everyone within the community, particularly those who have been marginalized, oppressed, or harmed. These approaches allow us to act and respond in ways that are healing rather than alienating or coercive.[10]

Thus, when we embrace RJE, we are more concerned with people getting what they need for healing and justice than about what they deserve. As we consider how RJE helps us address harm and conflict, a primary principle is a focus on underlying needs.

Addressing the Needs of All Involved

RJ emerged in response to a criminal justice system where too often the needs of those who have been harmed are ignored as the system takes on the role of victim. The same thing often happens in schools. Policies are designed to punish the student who breaks the rules, without often considering the needs of the person, or people, who are impacted by conflict or harm. RJE seeks to ensure that when harm occurs, the needs of those who have been impacted are met in ways that restore what has been broken, whether that is their sense of self, a relationship, or the hope that the school environment is still a safe place for them.

Return to the conflict analysis diagram that you completed (Figure 6.1). Think about the needs that are represented by the harms. Some of those needs can and should be met in a classroom environment, while others cannot. Sometimes teachers and school personnel either are not equipped or do not have the resources to address the needs that students bring to school with them or that they experience at school. For example, a student with a high ACE score might need more than support from educators; he might need professional counseling as well. However, educators can and should play a role in helping students find and access appropriate supports by making referrals to service providers.

At the core of repairing harms from an RJE perspective is a concern for the needs of each person involved.

Making Things Right

RJE attempts to make things right to the extent possible. The goals are repairing what is broken and restoring what has been harmed. In some cases, making things right may be in the form of restitution. For example, if a student vandalizes a teacher's car out of anger and frustration, we want to find out the context—what was the student responding to? Another priority, however, is to make things right for the teacher. People who are harmed often feel disempowered. Giving them an opportunity to make decisions about repairing harm allows them to regain a sense of control. In the preceding example, if the teacher requested that the student work toward paying for the damaged vehicle, the physical damage, as well as an emotional need for stability, would be repaired.

In other cases, making things right is less clear. How do you repair trust that has been broken? How do we restore a sense of dignity that has been violated or someone's sense of worth? These are critical questions that can be answered only in the context of the community.

Dennis Sullivan and Larry Tifft argue that when people who have caused harm are given an opportunity to make things right, it creates the possibility for them to "transcend the script" of negative identity often attached to those who cause harm.[11] The opportunity to make things right is a more effective means of holding students accountable than merely punishing them.

Building Supportive Accountability

RJ has often been critiqued for being too soft and for letting students get away with disruptive behaviors.

91

Opponents fear that without significant enough consequences for negative behaviors, chaos will result,
ultimately interfering with learning. In reality, RJ
does emphasize accountability. However, in RJE,
accountability is not about being *held* accountable
for certain behaviors, making the individual a passive recipient of someone else's decisions. Instead,
RJE promotes accountability *to* one's community,
supporting people as they take responsibility through
intentional actions that repair what was harmed
or violated. Within an RJE community, everyone is
accountable to a shared set of expectations and to
others within that community. Further, within an
RJE framework, accountability takes place within
a supportive community, which allows those in the
community to maintain their sense of belonging and
dignity even when they have caused harm (refer to
Figure 5.1).

Consider a situation in which other staff members
overhear a teacher berating a colleague. There are
often no formal rules against this type of behavior,
so requiring that the teacher be held accountable
for her words is unlikely. Within an RJE community,
however, there would be a place for acknowledging
the berating as a violation of dignity and creating an
opportunity for holding the teacher accountable to
an established faculty ethos of nurturing relationships. In addition, both teachers would have the
opportunity through some type of restorative process,
such as a talking circle, for receiving support from
other members of the teaching community while
they worked through their conflict. To this end,
RJE moves beyond merely restoring relationships to

transforming them. The Ontario Secondary School Teachers' Federation has been a leader in providing mediation services in exactly this arena. Its twelve mediators facilitate restorative dialogues with members experiencing conflict with other members. Established in 2001, the requests for restorative processes within this unique model grow every year. Anecdotal evidence is strong that when these meetings shift from solely "rights-based" to "relationship-based" interests, relationships become stronger through the process, and individuals report feeling a much better connection to their educational communities. The presenting issues that necessitated the mediation are addressed and do not reappear.

Transforming Conflict

Transforming conflict means addressing the immediate situation and *at the same time* building capacity to strengthen relationships. Without conflict, needs may remain unmet and harm may go unacknowledged. Returning to the analogy of the plant, biologists agree that wind and heavy rain that seem to be so destructive for a plant can actually serve to strengthen root and stem systems, therefore building resilience in the plant.

The transformative potential of conflict is consistent with some of our best understanding about how we learn. Jean Piaget, a developmental psychologist, built a theory of learning around the concepts of equilibrium and disequilibrium. Only when learners experience disequilibrium do they adapt and build new understanding or revise outdated ideas. In the same way, learning doesn't happen without the conflict of ideas. For example, Ben has experienced bullying by football players. He develops a perception of *all* football players as mean, violent, and aggressive. Jeffrey is on the football team and in Ben's fifth period class. Ben automatically dislikes Jeffrey. They experience conflict in class. Through an RJE process, Ben adjusts his perception about football players. The conflict became an opportunity to learn.

Likewise, John Dewey, a progressive educational philosopher, talked about the essential role that conflict plays in creating new ideas and ingenuity, claiming, "Conflict is the gadfly of thought . . . It shocks us out of sheep-like passivity."[12] Conflict doesn't always do this, he went on to say, but if we know that it can stir up new thoughts, we can embrace its transformative potential. RJE practitioners welcome conflict, believing that when we bring conflict to the fore, a community can work collaboratively to solve the problems *of* the community *within* the community.

> Think about a time when you experienced conflict and came through it stronger, wiser, or more resilient. Consider what enabled you to grow as a result of the conflict.

Another way that RJE transforms conflict is by creating opportunities to build social-emotional capacities, such as empathetic listening, self-regulation, problem solving, and perspective taking. In *The Little Book of Circle Processes,* Kay Pranis notes that being in talking circles together allows participants to

94

articulate and practice their core beliefs and values. Values for nurturing relationships emerge, such as honoring another's perspective, listening respectfully, and speaking one's own truth. In our own experience, we have found circle processes to be a thriving place of transformation. In order for transformative experiences to happen, however, we need to return to our discussion of justice and equity.

Addressing Justice and Equity

RJE holds a deep commitment to creating just and equitable learning environments. Further, it resists hierarchical relationships that rely on *power over* rather than *power with*. Thus, another way that RJE works to repair harm and transform conflict is by repairing those relationships that have been damaged by injustice. When educators feel, for example, that they have little choice in curriculum or instructional decisions, they may experience that lack of power as an injustice. Educators might seek to rectify that injustice by grasping at power over their students through what we call "trickle-down bullying."

Trickle-down bullying is a concept that implies that when someone in power over us uses that power in coercive ways, our tendency is to grasp for power from somewhere else. Sometimes that grasping for power comes at the expense of someone with less power than us. For example, school administrators may feel powerless in the face of so many regulations and grasp for power by placing pressure on teachers to get test scores up. Teachers, feeling a lack of empowerment, grab for power over their students, who then grasp for power over other students. Within this model, bullying becomes a structural phenomenon, one that we will likely not fix through bullying prevention programs. RJE seeks to restore a sense of agency to administrators, teachers, and students so that each experiences just and equitable relationships.

Within an RJE framework, repairing harm and making things right are about restoring balance and a sense of harmony and justice. This will require addressing the injustices that marginalized groups have felt for generations. Oppression and injustice must be addressed if we are truly going to repair harm and transform conflict. In his essay on student resistance to learning, Herbert Kohl[13] differentiates between those students who *can't* learn and those who *won't* learn. For some students, the act of "not learning" is one way that they can push back against a system that they deem is unfair and unjust. RJE approaches will likely be ineffective until we develop a critical consciousness about the harmful impacts of

- racism,
- classism,
- sexism,
- homophobia,
- colonialism, and
- other forms of oppression.[14]

According to Denise Breton,[15] an author and the director of Living Justice Press, RJ begins when those who have committed harms acknowledge their actions, take responsibility, and begin to work to make things right. Tracing the history of colonization that has characterized North America, she goes on to argue that it doesn't make sense to hold an indigenous person "accountable for drug possession or stealing a car while we fail to hold ourselves [as settlers] accountable for genocide that we committed so we could steal an entire state's worth of land." If we are serious about RJE, addressing historical harms and conflicts has to be part of our work.

Concrete Action Steps for Repairing Harm and Transforming Conflict

Being proactive in creating school climates where the well-being of *every* member is sought requires that RJE facilitators return over and over to the core beliefs of interconnectedness, worth, and the well-being of all participants. The following are specific ways that schools can build on those beliefs and begin to move toward the potential of RJE to repair harm and transform conflict.

Create Systems and Structures for Addressing Harm and Conflict

Creating structural supports for RJE is one way to ensure that addressing harm and conflict becomes a part of the culture of a school. Many schools already have peer mediation programs, anti-bullying programs, or SEL (social-emotional learning) initiatives. These are great places to begin connecting the principles of RJE to already existing structures. Ensuring that there is access to support resources—either on campus or through community-based providers—can help address individuals' needs. For example, one school designated an area of the school as a student support center. The counselors' offices, the nurse's office, and academic tutoring were all located there, making access to support easy for students. Students also knew that they could go to a small conference room there to work through conflicts. Trained RJE volunteers staffed the student support center twice a week and were available to facilitate circles or conferences.

Rethink School Discipline Systems

School discipline systems should be redesigned in ways that are supportive of RJE values and do not create further harm. Ongoing opportunities to participate in circle processes (i.e., circles of support and accountability, student conferencing, and reentry practices)[13] can support students and adults who exhibit more challenging behaviors.

Suspensions and/or expulsions should be used only in extreme or severe situations, be weighed on a case-by-case basis, and include a plan for reintegration. Reentry talking circles are non-punitive ways for rebuilding relationships and providing support. Replacing out-of-school suspensions with in-school suspensions can be a better option, as long as the in-school suspension room provides opportunities for RJE processes.

What if the in-school suspension room was reframed as a student support room where

- trained circle facilitators (peers and/or adults) could assist students working through conflict, while at the same time teaching them about problem-solving skills?
- counselors could work with students to develop greater social and emotional capacities?

- academic support is provided, recognizing the link between academic failure and behavior?
- circle processes provide opportunities for students and staff to express frustrations and harms in ways that lead to healing of relationships?

In addition, consider replacing the school's student conduct code with some type of community agreement in which all members of the community—administrators, students, teachers, and staff—agree to a shared set of expectations about how to be together. Rather than adults holding students accountable for things they themselves are not living into, a community agreement sends a message that adults and students alike are expected to live by restorative values.

Prepare Facilitators to Address Serious Harm

Facilitating circle processes when serious harm is involved requires preparation and experience. Facilitators need to be well trained in working with conflict, harm, and trauma. Facilitating circle processes or conferences in these situations is not as simple as putting people in a room together and having them talk it out. Without knowing how to facilitate, including adequately preparing participants in advance, there is a risk of revictimization and of creating more harm.

In our work with schools implementing RJE practices, we have heard too many stories of educators attempting to facilitate circle processes after only a few hours of training. In one situation, a teacher brought together two boys who had been in a fight. Not understanding the context and failing to do any type of pre-conferencing, one boy began bullying the other boy in the circle process, causing further harm and casting doubt on the potential of RJE to resolve conflicts. In another situation, a student, believing the circle was a safe place, began to open up emotionally about something personal. An unprepared facilitator, uncomfortable with the emotional response, exerted *power over* the student by interrupting the sharing and making suggestions. The facilitator's response violated the safe place and embarrassed the student in front of peers. Thus, we recommend that schools have several highly trained people (teachers, administrators, or community members) on hand with enough experience to facilitate circles for incidents of serious harm.

Summary

Repairing harm and transforming conflict are important components of RJE. When we prioritize healthy relationships and the dignity of each person, we are on the way to establishing restorative school cultures.

SECTION 3
Sustainable Growth

Restorative justice in education (RJE) has incredible potential for anchoring society in beliefs and values that create well-being. As we conclude this Little Book, we leave you with a variety of suggestions and resources to help you nurture strong foundational root systems and healthy growth. Chapter 7 provides a list of suggestions for beginning sustainable RJE work. The two appendices provide resources and references that will assist you as you seek to learn more. These final insights, gleaned from years of work across North America, are still only a beginning. We are excited to see the growth that will take place in the next decades.

Chapter 7:
A Tale of Two Schools: Thoughts about Sustainability

Provided in this chapter are two case studies of schools that have implemented RJE, one of which could be seen as successful, the other unsuccessful. As you read the descriptions of the two schools, list the differences you see between their approaches to implementing RJE.

Eastpoint Community School developed a five-year plan to integrate RJE into its school culture. It included ongoing professional development; student leadership; and a focus on developing skills, in-depth knowledge, and a restorative ethos. At the end of the five years, new student and staff support systems had been implemented:

- Students, teachers, administrators, families, and communities were experiencing improved relationships at school.
- RJE policies had been developed.

- Suspension rates were down by 45 percent.
- Graduation rates had improved by 30 percent.
- The district asked representatives from Eastpoint to begin working with other schools to lead district-wide implementation.

Sprucedale Regional School also developed a five-year plan. It included an initial training for all employees, with additional trainings for new employees each year. Restorative justice (RJ) practices were written into the student discipline code, and teachers were encouraged to include circle processes to build community in their classes. By the fifth year, the following had occurred:

- Most teachers had quit using circle processes, claiming that they were taking up too much time and were not effective for building community.
- Suspension rates were down, but teachers expressed frustration because nothing ever happened to students who were sent to the office.
- There was a general consensus among the students, teachers, administrators, families, and communities that RJE at Sprucedale was not working.

What were the differences between the two schools? Many factors played into the two very different outcomes. The key difference between Eastpoint and Sprucedale was the depth of understanding of RJE. We see this in how Eastpoint

- viewed RJE as a holistic approach to school culture rather than just a discipline system.

- integrated theory and practice, and did not simply focus on skills development.
- infused RJE into already existing systems rather than as a separate, tacked-on program.
- had ongoing, rather than one-time, professional development.

Restorative justice in education is a comprehensive and holistic approach to education. The types of change that we believe RJE can bring about are not limited to reductions in suspension rates, improved student behavior, or even improved academic achievement, although those outcomes are certainly included. What we hope for is the transformation of school cultures such that all members of the learning community—including students, teachers, staff, administrators, parents, and caregivers—feel that they belong. We long for schools where students and teachers are engaged in active and enthusiastic learning and where everyone—regardless of their race, gender, sexual orientation, ethnicity, religion, language, ability, or class—is valued and provided with what they need to grow and learn. Cultural transformation is possible only when RJE is implemented in a context where people are honored as worthy and interconnected.

As we have worked with and learned from schools across North America, we have been able to see restorative justice succeed and fail. Based on our research, practice, interactions, and conversations with schools across North America, we have observed schools where changes occurred but where the program fell apart when one particular RJ advocate retired. We have seen places where the entire school system was trained in restorative justice practices, but when continued professional development and support were not available, teachers became discouraged and quit using RJ practices. In short, if our work as restorative justice educators is to be sustainable, we have to build programs that lay strong foundations and provide wide, deep root systems. Extending the analogy of the plant with which we began, the trees represented on the cover of this book are able to grace the landscape because they have robust root systems that are at least as large as their crowns above the ground.

It is our hope that RJE moves from the margins to the mainstreams of education, gracing the landscape. For this to be accomplished, we offer the following recommendations for increasing the sustainability of RJE:

- *Never forget the seed and the roots.* Regularly engage with the core beliefs and values through activities and action. Take moments and longer time periods to creatively explore how nurturing institutional relational culture permeates all aspects of the school climate. Nurture the root system at every stage of development.
- *Start slowly and confidently.* Invite people to engage. People support change at different rates when they feel honored and respected and when they realize that the core beliefs and values resonate with their own. Though whole school implementation is ideal, this will occur only when individuals see the connection to themselves. Start with members of the school community who are convinced and

grow from there. Realize that our dominant models for implementing change are hierarchical and often do not model relational, restorative beliefs and values.

- *Model continually and consistently.* If you are supporting RJE implementation, model the ethos, values, and principles in all you do. If you hope for students to treat one another with respect and dignity, the adults must treat one another this way. Begin by implementing circle processes in staff and other adult meetings. Experiencing circles as adults first will help implement a relational ethos with students.

- *Provide ongoing professional development opportunities that focus on both underlying beliefs and values as well as specific skills.* Recognize that the term *training* can denote a skills-based experience and lead educators to conclude that RJE is a strategy for their "classroom management toolbox." Though skills are necessary, "educating" about the RJE ethos is required for transformational change. Sometimes this professional development can be provided internally by colleagues, students, or parents who are engaging with RJE. At other times, external expertise will propel implementation forward.

- *Don't do it alone.* If you are the RJE champion in your context, organize an RJE implementation team as soon as possible. Consider teachers, parents, caregivers, students, staff, and community members who are curious or committed to exploring with you. Be sure there are both "insiders," people who know the context of the school well,

107

and "outsiders," those who may be able to see the context from a different angle.

- *Be intentional.* As a team, begin by taking six to twelve months to become knowledgeable about restorative justice. Study, read, and participate in professional development. Visit other places where RJE is working well and learn from those schools. Make a careful plan. Don't forget to examine the current vision and mission of the school as these often already use the language of well-being. Demonstrate how RJE can support what already exists. Monitor and evaluate the plan to ensure that you are staying on track. As you grow, examine current policies for places that may be undermining RJE (e.g., most student codes of conduct include lists of behavioral consequences that disregard restoration). Don't forget to practice relational, restorative processes in your meetings.
- *Start with the assets you have.* What is already happening at your school that reflects RJE beliefs and values? Celebrate these assets and then expand. Identify what is happening that contradicts RJE. How can you use your assets to make changes?
- *Remember the power of youth leadership.* Engage children and youth as soon as possible. When they are given opportunities and support to take on leadership roles, they have the potential to deeply strengthen the culture of the school. See page 115 for schools where effective youth leadership has been a priority.

A word about resources: Make use of any financial resources to appoint full-time RJE coordinators who can provide internal professional development and facilitate circles for serious harm and conflict. However, where funds are not available, reconfigure current roles so that existing staff can provide consistency and leadership. Funding should not determine the degree to which you hold tightly to the values and principles of RJE; it is not about adding a program, but about gradually changing what already exists. It will be beneficial if people in specific roles in the school (e.g., curriculum programs, student life, guidance, discipline, etc.) are included early so they can initiate whole-school change. Regardless of the availability of resources, the plan must always include creating a strong foundational team that will remain intact over time and when change occurs (e.g., when supportive administrators or lead teachers leave).

Restorative justice in education is not a program; it's a framework. Eleven years after Lorraine Stutzman Amstutz and Judy Mullet's book *The Little Book of Restorative Discipline for Schools,* we amplify and strengthen what it provided—that restorative justice is a philosophy:

> "[W]e don't propose a cookie-cutter approach to restorative discipline; to imply such would over-simplify complex and diverse community situation. Rather, a restorative approach is a philosophy or framework that can guide us as we design programs and make decisions within our particular settings."

What develops in your context will be unique. What it will share with others who are implementing a restorative justice culture is a root system—the common belief and understanding of humanity as being worthy and interconnected. What we provide in this Little Book is a careful exploration of those roots so you can strengthen the growth of RJE where you are.

Resources

The following resources are recommended for implementing sustainable RJE. This list is not exhaustive, but will provide resources for getting started.

Books

Boyes-Watson, C., and K. Pranis. 2015. *Circle forward*. St. Paul, MN: Living Justice Press.

Boyes-Watson, C., and K. Pranis. 2010. *Heart of hope*. St. Paul, MN: Living Justice Press.

Claassen, R., and R. Claassen. 2008. *Discipline that restores*. South Carolina: BookSurge Publishing.

Claassen, R., and R. Claassen. 2015. *Making things right: Activities that teach restorative justice, conflict resolution, mediation, and discipline that restores*. North Charleston, SC: BookSurge Publishing.

Hendry, R. 2009. *Building and restoring respectful relationships in schools: A guide to using restorative practice*. Abingdon, UK: Routledge.

Holtham, J. 2009. *Taking Restorative Justice to Schools: A Doorway to Discipline*. Del Hayes Press.

Hopkins, B. 2004. *Just schools: A whole school approach to restorative justice*. London: Jessica Kingsley Publishers.

Hopkins, B. 2011. *The restorative classroom: Using restorative approaches to foster effective learning.* London: Optimus Education.

Karp, D. 2013. *The little book of restorative justice for colleges and universities.* Intercourse, PA: Good Books.

Morrison, B. 2007. *Restoring safe school communities: A whole school response to bullying, violence and alienation.* Sydney, Australia: The Federation Press.

Pranis, K. 2005. *The little book of circle processes: A new/old approach to peacemaking.* Intercourse, PA: Good Books.

Pranis, K., B. Stuart, and M. Wedge. 2003. *Peacemaking circles: From crime to community.* St. Paul, MN: Living Justice Press.

Riestenberg, N. 2012. *Circle in the square: Building community and repairing harm in school.* St. Paul, MN: Living Justice Press.

Sellman, E., H. Cremin, and G. McCluskey. 2013. *Restorative approaches to conflict in schools: Interdisciplinary perspectives on whole school approaches to managing relationships.* Abingdon, UK: Routledge.

Stutzman Amstutz, L., and J. H. Mullet. 2005. *The little book of restorative discipline for schools.* Intercourse, PA: Good Books.

Thorsborne, M., and P. Blood. 2013. *Implementing restorative practice in schools: A practical guide to transforming school communities.* London: Jessica Kingsley Publishers.

Wadhwa, Anita. 2015. *Restorative Justice in Urban Schools: Disrupting the School-to-Prison Pipeline.* London, Routledge Press.

Yoder, C. 2007. *The little book of trauma healing.* Intercourse, PA: Good Books.

Zehr, H. 1990. *Changing lenses: A new focus for crime and justice.* Scottdale, PA: Herald Press.

Zehr, H. 2002. *The little book of restorative justice.* Intercourse, PA: Good Books.

Zehr, H. 2002. Journey to belonging, in *Restorative justice: Theoretical foundations,* eds. E. G. M Weitekamp and H. J. Kerner, 23–25. Cullompton, UK: Willan Publishing.

Organizations and Websites

Adverse Childhood Experiences: http://www.cdc.gov/violenceprevention/acestudy/index.html

Center for Restorative Justice (Suffolk University): http://www.suffolk.edu/college/centers/14521.php

Center for Restorative Justice and Peacebuilding (University of Minnesota): http://www.cehd.umn.edu/ssw/RJP/default.asp

Center for Restorative Process: http://www.centerfor-restorativeprocess.com/

Community Justice for Youth Institute (Chicago): http://cjyiorg.publishpath.com/cjyi-services

Discipline That Restores (Fresno Pacific University): http://disciplinethatrestores.org/

Fix School Discipline: http://www.fixschooldiscipline.org

Institute for Restorative Justice and Restorative Dialogue (University of Texas): http://www.utexas.edu/research/cswr/rji/index.html

Minnesota Department of Education Restorative Practices: http://www.education.state.mn.us/MDE/SchSup/SchSafety/RestorativePractices/index.html

Project on Restorative Justice (Skidmore College):
http://www.skidmore.edu/campusrj/

Relationships First: Restorative Justice in Education:
http://relationshipsfirstnl.com/

Restorative Circles: http://www.restorativecircles.org/

Restorative Justice International (Fresno Pacific University):
http://www.restorativejusticeinternational.com/

Restorative Justice for Oakland Youth (RJOY): http://
rjoyoakland.org/

Restorative Justice Online: http://www.restorativejus-
tice.org/

Restorative Works Learning Network: http://restor-
ativeworks.net/

SaferSanerSchools: http://www.safersanerschools.org/

Zehr Institute of Restorative Justice (Eastern Mennonite
University): https://emu.edu/now/restorative-justice/

Professional Development and/or Education

Many of the websites listed in the preceding section offer professional development videos and information. In addition, these opportunities exist for more formal education:

The Center for Justice and Peacebuilding at Eastern Mennonite University offers a master's degree and an 18-hour certificate in restorative justice. It also regularly offers webinars, workshops, and summer courses: http://www.emu.edu/cjp/restorative-justice/%20/

Eastern Mennonite University Master's of Education Department offers a concentration in restorative justice in education, as well as a 15-hour

graduate certificate in restorative justice in education:
http://www.emu.edu/maed/

The International Institute for Restorative Practices
(IIRP) offers graduate degrees in restorative practices in addition to ongoing professional development: http://www.iirp.edu/

Simon Fraser University offers two certificate programs in restorative justice, one of foundational
and one with an education focus: https://www.sfu.
ca/continuing-studies/courses/crj/restorative-jus-
tice-in-educational-settings.html.

National, State/Provincial, and Regional Organizations

Central Virginia Restorative Justice: http://www.cen-
tralvirginiarj.org/

Colorado Restorative Justice: http://www.rjcolorado.
org/

Community Justice Initiatives: Educating for Peacebuilding:
http://www.cjibc.org/peacebuilding_program

International Institute for Restorative Practices:
http://www.iirp.edu/

National Association for Community and Restorative
Justice: http://www.nacrj.org/

Restorative Justice Institute of Maine: http://www.
rjimaine.org/

Restorative Justice Project of the Midcoast: http://
www.rjpmidcoast.org/

St. Croix Valley Restorative Justice: http://www.scvrjp.
org/

The Restorative Way: http://www.therestorativeway.
org/

School-Based RJE Programs

Baltimore City Schools Conflict Resolution Programs: http://www.communityconferencing.org/

Baltimore Curriculum Project: http://baltimorecp.blogspot.com/2012/01/bcp-and-restorative-practices-transform.html

California Conference for Equality and Justice: http://www.cacej.org/cause/restorative-justice/

Denver Public Schools: http://denver.co.schoolwebpages.com/education/dept/dept.php?sectionid = 164&

Fairfax County (VA) Public Schools RJ Program: http://www.fcps.edu/dss/ips/ssaw/violenceprevention/rj/

Minnesota Department of Education: http://www.education.state.mn.us/MDE/SchSup/SchSafety/RestorativePractices/index.html

Oakland (CA) Unified School District RJ Program: http://www.ousd.k12.ca.us/restorativejustice

San Francisco United School District: http://www.sfusd.edu/en/about-sfusd/strategic-plans-and-projects/2408.html

Endnotes

Preface

1. *Disproportionality* refers to the overrepresentation of some groups of students within school discipline systems, leading to higher suspension and expulsion rates and contributing to what has been termed "the school-to-prison pipeline," a phenomenon that shows that students with higher suspension rates are more likely to end up incarcerated.

2. Gregory, A., K. Clawson, A. Davis, and J. Gerewitz. 2014. The promise of restorative practices to transform teacher-student relationships and achieve equity in school discipline. *Journal of Educational and Psychological Consultation* 25: 1–29.

3. Skiba, R. J., M. I. Arredondo, and M. K. Rausch. 2014. New and developing research on disparities in discipline. *Discipline Disparities Series.* Bloomington, IN: The Equity Project at Indiana University.
   Morgan, E., N. Saloman, M. Plotkin, and R. Cohen. 2014. *School Discipline Consensus Report.* New York: Council of State Governments Justice Center.
   Vaandering, D. 2011. A faithful compass: Rethinking the term restorative justice to find clarity. *Contemporary Justice Review* 14(3):307–28.

Chapter 1

1. This holistic definition of justice draws on ancient and contemporary indigenous and spiritual traditions—in particular, the broad understanding of circle

connectedness and justice as the "good way" and the Judeo-Christian concepts of *shalom* and covenant. See Chapter 4.

Bianchi, H. 1994. *Justice as sanctuary.* Bloomington, IN: Indiana University Press.

Hadley, M. 2001. *The spiritual roots of restorative justice.* Albany, NY: SUNY Press.

McCaslin, W. 2005. *Justice as healing: Indigenous ways: Writings on community peacemaking and restorative justice from the Native Law Centre.* St. Paul, MN: Living Justice Press.

Pranis, K., B. Stuart, and M. Wedge. 2003. *Peacemaking circles: From crime to community.* St. Paul, MN: Living Justice Press.

Ross, R. 1996. *Returning to the teachings.* Toronto: Penguin.

Wolterstorff, N. 2008. *Justice: Rights and wrongs.* Princeton, NJ: Princeton University Press.

Zehr, H. 2005. *Changing lenses: A new focus for crime and justice,* 3rd ed. Waterloo, IA: Herald Press.

2. Pranis, K. 2005. *The little book of circle processes: A new/ old approach to peacemaking,* 24. Intercourse, PA: Good Books.

   All of the books relating to restorative justice in the Little Book Series identify in various ways this philosophical foundation for restorative justice. This Little Book seeks to highlight the importance of this philosophy.

3. Recent educational reform movements, particularly in the United States, place a great deal of pressure on schools to improve test scores, often with serious consequences for failing to do so. Curricular decisions are often made with testing in mind, rather than students, creating a narrow curriculum that is primarily test-driven. This excessive use of testing as a way to measure and rank both students and teachers, as well as schools and districts, distracts from relational pedagogy espoused by restorative justice. For more about testing, see:

Robinson, Ken. 2010. "Changing education paradigms." http://www.ted.com/talks/ken_robinson_changing_ education_paradigms

4. Morrison, B. 2010. From social control to social engagement: Enabling the "time and space" to talk through restorative justice and responsive regulation, in *Contemporary Issues in Criminology Theory and Research,* Eds. R. Rosenfeld, K. Quinet, and C. Garcia, 97–106. Belmont, CA: Wadsworth Cengage Learning.

Chapter 2

1. For information regarding indigenous and spiritual roots of justice and peacebuilding, we suggest:

   Hadley, M. 2001. *The spiritual roots of restorative justice.* Albany, NY: SUNY Press.

   McCaslin, W. (Ed.) 2005. *Justice as healing: Indigenous ways.* St. Paul, MN: Living Justice Press.

   Pranis, K., B. Stuart, and M. Wedge. 2003. *Peacemaking circles: From crime to community.* St. Paul, MN: Living Justice Press.

   Ross, R. 1996. *Returning to the teachings.* Toronto: Penguin.

2. For information about the history of VORP and VOC, see:

   Sullivan, D., and L. Tifft. 2006. *Handbook of restorative justice: A global perspective.* Milton Park, UK: Routledge.

3. Skiba, R. J. 2000. *Zero tolerance, zero evidence: An analysis of school disciplinary practice.* Bloomington, IN: Indiana Education Policy Center.

4. Anderson, C. L. 2004. Double jeopardy: The modern dilemma for juvenile justice. *University of Pennsylvania Law Review* 152(3): 1181–1219.

5. CBC. April 13, 2007. Ontario agrees to end zero-tolerance school policy. http://www.cbc.ca/news/ canada/toronto/ontario-agrees-to-end-zero-tolerance-school-policy-1.671464.

6. American Psychological Association. 2008. Are zero tolerance policies effective in the schools? An evidentiary review and recommendations. *American Psychologist* 63(9): 852–62.

7. U.S. Department of Education, Office for Civil Rights. October 26, 2010. Dear colleague letter: Harassment and bullying. http:// www2.ed.gov/about/offices/list/ocr/letters/colleague-201010.html.

8. Morrison, B., and D. Vaandering. 2012. Restorative justice: Pedagogy, praxis, and discipline. *Journal of School Violence* 11(2).

9. https://education.waikato.ac.nz/resources-for-schools/

10. https://emu.edu/maed/restorative-justice/

11. http://www.sfu.ca/continuing-studies/programs-and-courses/area-of-study/community-building/restorative-justice.html

Chapter 3

1. Zehr, H. 1990. *Changing lenses: A new focus for crime and justice*. Scottdale, PA: Herald Press.

2. Pajares, M. F. 1992. Teachers' beliefs and educational research: Cleaning up a messy construct. *Review of Educational Research* 62(3): 307-32.
Willard, D. 1999. Spiritual formation meets the gospel. Vancouver: Regent College Lectures.

3. This discussion regarding Western neoliberalism and RJ is articulated well in:
Llewellyn, K. and J. Llewellyn. 2015. A restorative approach to learning: Relational theory as feminist pedagogy in universities, in *Feminist Pedagogy in Higher Education: Critical Theory and Practice*, Eds. T. Light, J. Nicholas, and R. Bondy, 11–32. Waterloo, IA: Wilfrid Laurier University Press.

4. Boyes-Watson, C., and K. Pranis. 2015. *Circle forward*. St. Paul, MN: Living Justice Press.

Pranis, K. 2007. *Circle processes*. Intercourse, PA: Good Books. Both ground their work on circle processes in a clear articulation of these beliefs that are expanded on with seven core assumptions.

5. These three values essential for relationship are identified in:
   Llewellyn, J. 2012. Restorative justice: Thinking relationally about justice, in *Being relational,* Eds. J. Downie and J. Llewellyn. Vancouver: UBC Press.

6. For more details, see:
   Vaandering, D. 2011. A faithful compass: Rethinking the term restorative justice to find clarity. *Contemporary Justice Review* 14(3): 307–28.
   Other questions could be asked to critically self-reflect, such as, "Am I focused on needs or punishment? Am I seeing this person as relational or independent? Am I respecting this person as unconditionally worthy? Am I creating conditions for this person's worth? The three questions chosen for this Little Book are suggested as a way to consistently expose how personal core beliefs align with the core beliefs of RJE. They also keep the focus on personal responsibility and do not allow for deflecting responsibility to others.

7. Morrison, B., and D. Vaandering. 2012. Restorative justice: Pedagogy, praxis, and discipline. *Journal of School Violence* 11(2): 138–55.

Chapter 4

1. For an in-depth discussion of the concepts of *shalom* and *sedeqah,* see:
   Marshall, C. 2005. *Little Book of Biblical Justice.* Intercourse, PA: Good Books.

2. Akrami, Amir. 2016. Yale Divinity School, personal correspondence.

3. Yazzie, R. "Life comes from it": Navajo justice concepts. https://www.amizade.org/wp-content/uploads/2011/07/LifeComesFromIt.doc.

4. Elliot, E. 2011. The geometry of individuals and relationships, in *Security with care,* 139. Blackpoint, NS: Fernwood Publishers.

5. Franklin, U., and M. Swenarchuk. 2006. *The Ursula Franklin reader.* Toronto: Between the Lines.

6. Boyes-Watson, C., and K. Pranis. 2015. *Circle forward,* 139. St. Paul, MN: Living Justice Press.

7. American Psychological Association. 2008. Are zero tolerance policies effective in the schools? An evidentiary review and recommendations. *American Psychologist* 63(9): 852–62.

Although we focused on the student in this example, it is important to consider the harm experienced by educators who are repeatedly expected to comply with policies, such as zero tolerance, that violate their own conscience.

8. Forty years of data demonstrate this disproportionality. See for example:

Fenning, P., and J. Rose. 2007. Overrepresentation of African American students in exclusionary discipline: The role of school policy. *Urban Education* 42(6): 536–59.

Gregory, A., R. J. Skiba, and P. A. Noguera. 2010. The achievement gap and the discipline gap: Two sides of the same coin? *Educational Researcher* 39(1): 59–68.

U.S. Department of Education, Office for Civil Rights. October 26, 2010. Dear colleague letter: Harassment and bullying. http:// www2.ed.gov/about/offices/list/ocr/letters/colleague-201010.html.

9. Standard VI reads: "Candidates demonstrate knowledge of how theories and research about social justice, diversity, equity, student identities, and schools as institutions can enhance students' opportunities to learn in English Language Arts." Located at www.ncte.org.

10. Sullivan, D., and L. Tifft. 2001. *Restorative justice: Healing the foundations of our everyday lives,* 167. Monsey, NY: Willow Tree Press.

11. For more information about addressing students' needs in schools, see:
    Deci, E. L., and R. M. Ryan. 1991. A motivational approach to self: Integration in personality. *Perspectives on motivation.* Lincoln, NE: University of Nebraska Press.

12. Glasser, W. 1985. Discipline has never been the problem and isn't the problem now. *Theory into Practice* 24(4): 241–46.

13. Zehr, H. 2002. Journey to belonging, in *Restorative justice: Theoretical foundations,* Eds. E. G. M. Weitekamp and H. J. Kerner, 23–25. Cullompton, UK: Willan Publishing.

14. Freire, P. 1970. *Pedagogy of the oppressed.* New York: Continuum Press.

15. Vygotsky, L. S. 1986. *Thought and language,* 39. Cambridge, MA: MIT Press.

16. See more about differentiation in:
    Tomlinson, C. A. 2014. *The differentiated classroom: Responding to the needs of all learners.* Alexandria, VA: ASCD.

17. For more information, see:
    Ladson-Billings, G. 1990. Culturally relevant teaching: Effective instruction for black students. *The College Board Review* 7(15): 20-25.
    Ladson-Billings, G. 1995. Toward a theory of culturally relevant pedagogy. *American Educational Research Journal* 32(3): 465–91.

18. Whitewashing refers to the practice of looking at diversity through the lens of the majority, without considering the perspectives of those who daily experience discrimination. If we really want to avoid

whitewashing, we need to create more spaces for marginalized youth to share their perspectives. More information about integrating equity into the curriculum can be found in:
Gorski, P., and Swalwell, K. 2015. Equity literacy for all. *Educational Leadership* 72(6): 34–40.

19. For example, see:
U.S. Department of Education, Office for Civil Rights. October 26, 2010. Dear colleague letter: Harassment and bullying. Retrieved from http:// www2.ed.gov/ about/offices/list/ocr/letters/colleague-201010.html.

20. The works of Paulo Freire and bell hooks create a framework for understanding RJE more broadly, both in concepts here in this chapter and in our understanding of the humanization of one another. See also: Vaandering, D. 2010. The significance of critical theory for restorative justice in education. *The Review of Education, Pedagogy, and Cultural Studies* 32(2):145–76.

21. Vaandering, D. 2010. The significance of critical theory for restorative justice in education. *The Review of Education, Pedagogy, and Cultural Studies* 32(2):145–76. In this article, Vaandering talks extensively about the hidden curriculum that exists when teachers are unaware of their implicit biases.

22. Ladson-Billings, G. 1995. Toward a theory of culturally relevant pedagogy. *American Educational Research Journal* 32(3): 465–91.

23. http://www.schooltalkdc.org/

24. http://specialedcoop.org/coop/

25. See also the I'm Determined program sponsored by the Virginia Department of Education: www.imdetermined.org/.

Chapter 5

1. Clinton, J. 2013. *The power of adult child relationships: Connection is the key.* Ontario: Queen's Printer for Ontario.

2. Boyes-Watson, C., and K. Pranis. 2015. *Circle forward,* 17–19. St. Paul, MN: Living Justice Press.
   It provides a similar but more detailed explanation of power in the context of RJE.

3. This matrix is a slight variation on several others. See for example:
   Vaandering, D. 2013. A window on relationships: Reflecting critically on a current restorative justice theory. *Restorative Justice: An International Journal* 1(3): 311-33.

4. Elliot, E. 2011. The geometry of individuals and relationships, in *Security with care.* Blackpoint, NS: Fernwood Publishers.
   This concept is the impetus behind using the reflective questions *Am I honoring, Am I measuring,* and *What message am I sending?* with all relationships identified in Figure 5.1. As each ripple is described, take a moment to ask these questions to critically assess your relationships and open up possibilities for change.

5. Vaandering, D. 2014. Relational restorative justice pedagogy in educator professional development. *Curriculum Inquiry* 44:4.
   Also see descriptive video of this concept at http://relationshipsfirstnl.com/video/.

6. Figure 5.2 used with permission. See:
   Vaandering, D. 2014. Relational restorative justice pedagogy in educator professional development. *Curriculum Inquiry* 44(4): 508-30.

7. Boyes-Watson, C., and K. Pranis. 2015. *Circle forward,* 23. St. Paul, MN: Living Justice Press.

Chapter 6

1. Zehr, H. 1990. *Changing lenses: A new focus for crime and justice,* 199. Scottdale, PA: Herald Press.

2. Casella, R. 2003. Zero tolerance policy in schools: Rationale, consequences, and alternatives. *Teachers College Record* 105(5): 872-92.

3. American Psychological Association. 2008. Are zero tolerance policies effective in the schools? An evidentiary review and recommendations. *American Psychologist* 63(9): 852–62.

4. The ACEs study looks at ten questions related to childhood experiences that potentially have a negative impact on emotional health. A person with a high ACE score has had multiple Adverse Childhood Experiences. See more information on the ACE Study here: http://www.cdc.gov/violenceprevention/acestudy/index.html.

5. Yoder, C. 2007. *The little book of trauma healing.* Intercourse, PA: Good Books.

6. Yehuda, R., N. P. Daskalakis, L. M. Bierer, et al. 2015. Holocaust exposure induced intergenerational effects on *FKBP5* methylation. *Biological Psychiatry* [advance online publication]. http://www.biological psychiatryjournal.com/article/S0006-3223(15) 00652-6/abstract

7. For more information about Walla Walla, consider hosting a viewing of the documentary *Paper Tigers.* More information can be found at http://www.papertigersmovie.com/.

8. Hicks, D. 2011. *Dignity: Its essential role in resolving conflict.* New Haven, CT: Yale University Press.

9. Zehr, H. 2002. *The little book of restorative justice,* 37. Intercourse, PA: Good Books.

10. Stutzman Amstutz, L., and J. H. Mullet. 2005. *The little book of restorative discipline for schools,* 15. Intercourse, PA: Good Books.

11. Sullivan, D., and L. Tifft. 2001. *Restorative justice: Healing the foundations of our everyday lives.* Monsey, NY: Willow Tree Press.

12. Dewey, J. 1922. Human nature and conduct: An introduction to social psychology. New York: Holt.

13. Kohl, H. 1995. *I won't learn from you.* New York: New Press.

14. Breton, D. 2012. Decolonizing restorative justice *Tikkun,* Winter 2012: 45–47.

15. Marcucci, O. February 2016. *The role of teacher buy-in in a restorative justice in a predominantly black school.* Paper presented at the Ethnography in Education Forum, Philadelphia, PA.

About the Authors

Katherine Evans is an assistant professor of education at Eastern Mennonite University in Virginia. Katherine helped develop EMU's graduate program in Restorative Justice in Education, which supports educators as they create more just and equitable educational opportunities for all students, including those marginalized based on race, ethnicity, income, ability, language, sexual orientation, and gender.

Dorothy Vaandering is an associate professor at the Faculty of Education at Memorial University in Newfoundland and Labrador. After an extensive career as a primary-elementary educator, she now researches the implementation and sustainability of restorative justice in education. She works passionately to integrate restorative justice philosophy into theory and practice in her current role as researcher and teacher-educator.